PRAISE FOR THE BLOG
STUFF DUTCH PEOPLE LIKE.COM

"Please do tell when this blog will be bundled up and published in a book. Absolute must have!" - **Lise**

"I was having a particularly bad day. Then of course I stumbled onto this blog and now I can't wipe the grin off my face. Thank you for making me feel better and 'gefeliciteerd' with your astute cultural ethnography of us Dutch folk. Relativism schmelativism!" - **bramiam**

"I am Dutch and I LOVE YOU! Hahaha keep up the good work!" **Joyce**

"This site is hilarious. I cried of laughter. I am Dutch myself and just everything is true what is said here! Very, very funny written!!!" - **Paula**

"I just can't believe how freaking funny, hilarious, informative and instructive this blog is! Including the comments. Big kudos from this cheesehead. My foreign girlfriend really has to read this." - **Joris**

"I Love your blog! Cause everything you write is soooo true. And, as a Dutch girl, it's so funny to read that the things we consider "normal" are so strange for other people. Every post makes me smile 3 kisses on the cheek." - **mamakimm**

"Hi there! OMG! I just can't believe that I JUST discovered your blog. It's like I'm reading my own life. I am a non-Dutch student living here for 2 years now. Every single word you write here is true. I just thought I was the only one who noticed these things… Good to know I'm not the only one. You make my life…"
- **Paulina**

"Just love it...all so true. After living abroad for 2.5 years I still haven't lost the Dutchness. Keep up the good work!" - **colocha**

"I teach an "Inburgeringsklas" myself and KNS (Kennis van de Nederlandse Samenleving; how Dutch act and react in their natural habitat) is one of the subjects I teach and needless to say: we always have a blast with your columns. The nosepicking is one of my faves' personally….." - **Marie-Anne**

"Your blog is hysterical! I am Dutch and have lived in the UK, The States and China for more than 10 years altogether and worked with people from many other cultures as I went along. I recognise so much of what you have written from what my friends and colleagues have told me they find remarkable about the Dutch. Your blog had me crying with laughter – very well perceived and so true. Uncanny. I look forward to the next entry already." - **EH**

"Hilarious Blog! I mailed the url to both my sisters in law (one is originally Welsh but living in the USA for 40 years and one is Canadian). Both are married to prototype Dutch brothers, living abroad for ages (herring, pils, boerenkool etc.) and they find themselves still amazed when the varnish peels off and yet another weird Dutch habit peeps out." - **rene**

"How I love this blog! Keep writing, there is much more monkeyness to explore!!"
- **Chocokaatje**

"Love this blog!!! How true, how funny!!" - **Maria**

"I want to thank the AD for writing an article about this blog!This website is now one of my top faves!" - **Safie**

"Dude… funniest shit I have read in a long time!!! Keep it up!" - **John**

STUFF DUTCH PEOPLE LIKE

A Celebration of the Lowlands
and its Peculiar Inhabitants

by Colleen Geske

Words by Colleen Geske
Design by Elisha Leo
Edits by Tricia & Allan Geske
Proofreading by Shelley Antscherl
And everything else by Moses Faleafaga

Published in the Netherlands by LATOUR PUBLISHING

Some of the material in this book originally appeared, in different form, on the popular blog StuffDutchPeopleLike.com

Photograph credits can be found on page 196

ISBN 978-90-821336-0-8

Printed in the Netherlands

10 9 8 7 6 5 4 3 2 1

www.stuffdutchpeoplelike.com
www.facebook.com/stuffdutchpeoplelike
www.twitter.com/stuffdutchlike

For media inquiries, corporate & volume sales or any other request, please contact us at stuffdutchpeoplelike@gmail.com

Stuff Dutch People Like

To all the Dutch people I've known and not-known;
thank you for the inspiration and your ability to laugh at yourselves.
My thanks also to the readers of the 'Stuff Dutch People Like' blog
for their endless opinions, support and good humour.

TABLE OF CONTENTS

1: Bicycles.. 3
2: Gezellig(heid).. 7
3: Hagelslag...12
4: Directness..15
5: Battling water..21
6: Three kisses..24
7: Orange..28
8: Not owning curtains...32
9: Tulips..36
10: Birthday congratulations 39
11: Discussing the weather 43
12: Lekker 46
13: Scheduling agenda appointments.................................49
14: Red pants 52
15: Natural birth..56
16: Zwarte Piet 61
17: Stroopwafel 68
18: Bring your own cake..70
19: Mashing their food (stamppot) 74
20: Skating (on natural ice).......................................79
21: Herring 82
22: Hair gel 85
23: Jokes about Germans and Belgians 88
24: Dairy..91
25: Going camping..94

26: Windmills …… 98

27: Picking their noses …… 101

28: Friet & mayo (french fries) …… 105

29: Licorice …… 108

30: Forcing drop on unsuspecting foreigners …… 111

31: Keeping it real …… 113

32: Names that sound ridiculous in English …… 117

33: King's Day (formerly Queen's Day) …… 122

34: Dat kan niet …… 125

35: Impossibly steep stairs …… 128

36. Sinterklaas …… 132

37: The Birthday Calendar …… 138

38: Not working/working …… 141

39: Cows that say "boo" …… 144

40: Tiny sinks with only cold water …… 147

41: Being Tall …… 151

42: Swearing with diseases …… 156

43: Speaking in expressions …… 160

44: White leggings …… 165

45: Beschuit met muisjes …… 168

46: Suspicious spreads …… 171

47: Normalcy: doe normaal …… 175

48: Delaying marriage …… 179

49: Infiltrating English …… 182

50: ? …… 185

INTRODUCTION

When I first started the 'Stuff Dutch People Like' blog in 2011 I had hoped that fellow expats and foreigners living in the Lowlands might give it a read. I had no idea that the Dutch themselves would embrace it in such numbers and propel the blog to such heights. I clearly misjudged Dutch people's sense of humour and their ability to laugh at themselves.

The day I hit 10,000 reader comments on the blog, I realised I had clearly struck a nerve. Maybe the Dutch never knew they were so special. Or maybe they just loved the chance to finally read (and write) about themselves. Regardless, Dutch people and the things they do and like are undeniably weird. And that weirdness clearly needed to be celebrated.

Discovering a new country and a new people is exhilarating, frustrating and inspiring all at once. It forces you to look at yourself in new ways, and realise you are forever changed. I'd like to think after 9 years of living in the Netherlands that I'm a bit Dutch too. I'll take your gezelligheid, work-life balance and even your directness. You can keep your drop, hagelslag, white leggings and your nose-picking.

I write about the Dutch in the same way you would tease a school crush on the playground, slightly taunting, but secretly with great affection.

Colleen Geske
Amsterdam, October 2013

ABOUT THIS BOOK

As the name implies, this book is a collection of stuff that Dutch people like.

For your reading pleasure we've compiled 50 of these items, in no particular order.

We've also included a selection of unedited comments made on the Stuff Dutch People Like blog. A blog is only as good as its commenters. And it turns out that ours are bloody genius. What they had to say was hilarious; too hilarious not to share. And so we did.

Happy reading.

#1 BICYCLES

You may have noticed more than a few wheeled contraptions whizzing by you in the Netherlands. In fact, it sometimes seems impossible to separate where the Dutch begin and their bicycles end. Rain (rain, and more rain) or shine, the Dutch can be found criss-crossing this bridged city on their trusty (and rusty) two-wheeled friends.

Of course, everyday cycling in itself is not such a special feat, but the Dutch certainly bring their own distinctive flair to the sport. Don't expect to see any fancy, sophisticated, titanium-suspension-rigged bicycles on the streets. Nope, the Dutch prefer their gearless, rusted, chain-just-barely-hanging-on variety. Why, you ask? Well, practicality and frugality run through every

Dutchie's blood. Why spend more for fancy features when your unusually strong thighs and lungs can make up for the rest? Heck, the Dutch even prefer to power their necessary bike lights with their own leg-pumping-power. A reliable solution at no extra cost!

35,000 KM
TOTAL LENGTH
OF BIKE PATHS

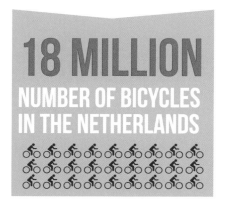

18 MILLION
NUMBER OF BICYCLES
IN THE NETHERLANDS

However, the most impressive feat of all is how Dutch people ride these heaps of metal and rust. Don't be surprised by their uncanny ability to ride a gearless bicycle while talking on a mobile phone, carrying 2 children, 6 bags of groceries, a television set, and a mattress! Having grown up on wheels, the Dutch conduct daily superhuman acts with laid-back coolness.

Wondering how you are ever going to avoid getting run over by a fervent cyclist? Unfortunately we don't have a lot of good advice for you there. Keep your eyes peeled, don't dare set foot on the bike paths, and if you accidently do, you'll be sure to hear an onslaught of angry bicycle bells.

With over 880,000 bicycles in a city of less than 790,000 people, you are sure to see some interesting spectacles on wheels!

WHAT OUR COMMUNITY HAS TO SAY

There is actually another reason why dutch people ride old, shabby-looking bikes: bikes get stolen very frequently, and new and fancy ones have a higher chance of getting stolen.

Mechelke

Outside the big cities most people do have more fancy type of bikes, just not in the big cities where the chance of the bikes being stolen is Q quite large.

Lisette

The crucial trick: if possible, put your bike next to a better-looking bike with worse locks.

Ilja

I'm currently learning to drive in the netherlands and the cyclists here are the biggest menace. They have zero respect for any road rules and they know that they can get away with anything... it's terrifying because you are left to juggle with their life because of their carelessness and incompetence. Never mind the fact some of them are mothers with babies strapped onto the front of the bike... then just running red lights etc. Hard to believe they can't see the danger.

Paulien

Sarah

TRUE! A And the reason is quite simple: b by law cyclists are protected A as the weaker party in case of a c collision with motorized traffic.

Patricia

As a dutchee i want to add that i love to ride my bicycle. And i have a couple of them for different purposes. One to drive to the store (with my child strapped in the back or in the front), one to race, one to do some mountain biking (not a lot of mountains in holland but you know what i mean...). My father and mother own even more bicycles. I think they add up to 10. They have different once for the winter and summer! But we will not take those bicycles for a spin in the city.... If i would take the "expensive" ones with me, I park them inside the house / office etc.

Christopher

Hehehe i'm just thinking of the ridiculous stuff i have done on a bike whilst cycling through town and it includes putting on or taking of a jacket whilst wearing a backpack. Unpacking my backpack/checking if i didn't forget something, taking pictures, filming, texting, calling, writing and drawing (on a full sized a4) and obviously eating a sandwich and drinking beer.

Ow and sleeping (Well nearly sleeping at least)... and i have never had/caused an accident (it is a miracle If i think about it)

#2 GEZELLIG

Spend any time in the Netherlands and you will quickly learn that Dutch people love this perplexing guttural-sounding word. The Dutch are fiercely proud of this word and everything it represents. *Gezelligheid* is the modern day religion of the Dutch. They love it, they need it, and, above all, they respect it.

The Dutch love to ask foreigners (over and over) if they know the word *gezellig.* Once you do know its meaning don't be surprised if you are then asked (over and over again) how to pronounce it. We suggest you learn to love it too, because the reality is you won't be able to escape it (or its pronunciation).

The tricky part about this word is that it has no precise English translation; cosy, quaint, comfortable, familiar and friendly all come up short. Simply put, gezellig is a feeling.

Things get even trickier to comprehend because Dutch people tend to evaluate just about everything on its particular level of *gezelligheid*. A place can be *gezellig*, a room can be gezellig, a person can be gezellig, an evening can be *gezellig*. Dutch women have even been known to describe birth as a *gezellig* experience!

There are, however, two sides to every coin. True to form, *ongezellig* is *gezellig's* nasty twin brother. *Ongezellig* is much sharper and can cut like a razor. "Let's get out of this place, it's just so *ongezellig*" sums it up like nothing else can.

The good news is that even if you stay in the Netherlands for only a short amount of time, *gezellig* and its accompanying state-of-mind are sure to rub off on you. You still might not be able to translate the word perfectly into your own language, but chances are one day it will suddenly dawn on you that the place, the company, or the moment you are in is truly *gezellig*, and that will be worth a thousand words – in any language!

WHAT OUR COMMUNITY HAS TO SAY

How does it differ from 'comfortable'? I tried putting that word in place every time you wrote 'gezellig' and the article still seemed to make sense.

Mu

Comfortable still doesn't quite cut it. It has a calm, homey quality. However, a lively party or an animated chat can also be gezellig – not really situations that would be described as "comfortable".In my opinion, gezellig mostly depends on people. Being all alone would never be described as gezellig, even if you're comfortable. You need (the right) company for a place or a situation to be gezellig.

Linda

I agree it mostly depends on people,but it is possible to be alone and be "gezellig" e.g. if one's house qualifies as such. I'm Dutch, my American wife tried to understand the "gezelligheid" concept. This is about nine years ago and we were in the NL watching the news about a village where the surroundings were completely flooded and, if not for an impromptu dike of sandbags, the village itself would have been flooded. They were interviewing a local woman who described living there at that moment as rather "gezellig". At the point my wife knew she would never quite understand the concept. It is most definitely not the equivalent of "comfortable".

Mark

A room can also be gezellig by the way it is furnished, A party can be gezellig. A dinner can be gezellig. You can have a gezellig chat with a friend, etc, No cozy does not cut it, but it is the closest we have in the English Language. I was born and raised in the Netherlands but have now live in the US for 40 years and am a teacher. There is no word exactly like gezellig.

Sonja

From what I've gathered, the word can be summed up by "a sense of coziness and belonging in one's present environment and company". It's not EXACTLY corresponding to the word "cozy", but it's most definitely related. It seems to be a sort of "vibe of coolness evoked by a cozy and welcoming environment". It's perfectly possible to "define" any word in any language on a meaningful level, meaning it is also perfectly possible to translate a word based on context. There are many valid candidates in English to "substitute", both single words and phrases that could convey the same general meaning.

Wohdin

A recent example: Last week I hosted Dutch friends (father + daughter) at my house who were on holiday. Because she was 14 yrs., I assumed that she would want separate sleeping quarters from her father, so I made her a bed in a separate guest room. When I showed her to her room, she asked me if she could sleep in the same room with her father. When I asked her why she would want to try and cram this mattress into a small (read: uncomfortable) space, she replied: "Het is meer gezellig!" (It is more gezellig).

Benny

I've looked up the word 'gezellig' in the online dictionary and they've come up with: cosy, snug, snugly, cozily, pleasant, sociable, chatty. However, as a Dutch person with English speaking friends, I've come to the conclusion that there is no English word to describe 'gezellig'. All the translations are apt to a different situation, but none are appropriate for how we Dutch use the word 'gezellig' in every situation. Often I find myself looking for the right word to describe the feeling I have when talking or meeting with English speaking friends, when if I were with Dutch speaking friends I would say: It was 'gezellig'. I think 'gezellig' should be used in every language LOL.

Tessa

Gezellig IS difficult translate precisely because – for Dutch people – the word has special feelings, circumstances and connotations attached to it and ingrained within it [...] It's very much like trying to precisely define a nation's 'sense of humour' ... you know and feel the difference in your gut ... but it's almost impossible to describe why one is better, funnier or different.

Robert

You know, it's funny that English hasn't absorbed "gezellig" the same way it has absorbed so many other foreign words, like shampoo, sorbet, and even schadenfreude. It must be that gutteral "g" that English-speakers find so "ongezellig".

Steve

Funerals are often gezellig, as it is a get-together of relatives who often haven't seen each other for a long time. After the funeral, there's usually coffee and sandwiches during which time people catch up. So yes, it can be gezellig. 'Leuk' has the same leve of insignificance. Everybody always says 'leuk'. Leuke jurk, leuk behang, leuke vakantie… It doesn't say anything about the dress, the wallpaper or the holidays. Why is it 'leuk'? Because the dress is red? Because the wallpaper suits te person? Because the weather was nice on holiday? It doesn't really mean anything.

Desirée

I have a love hate relationship with the word gezellig. Sometimes I really love the word. However, I really dislike how it's sometimes used for manipulation though. For example, if people are trying to pressure me into attending a social event (such as a circle party, or somewhere really loud and crowded) that I don't want to go to, they start with grilling me on why I don't want to go. Even if I can give 40 valid reasons, their response is invariably "Maar, het is toch gezellig!".

Tja

I'm sorry but every time dutch people call something 'gezellig', it happens to be the most boring time on earth, and the leuke people and leuke (superficial) conversation makes me quite frustrated. I wonder if they say it to convince themselves that they are having a good time?I think it is also cultural. Dutch people like to *describe* elaborately the time they are having. In a lot of other cultures, people don't see the need to state that they are having a good time while they are having a good time, as this would be redundant.I suspect that inside they are not having a good time at all..

Steve

#3 HAGELSLAG

Of all the Dutch edible eccentricities, *hagelslag* tops the list. *Hagelslag* is the Dutch version of sprinkles. In most countries, sprinkles are primarily reserved to fancifully top the likes of ice-cream and birthday cake for children. In the Netherlands however, it is apparently perfectly normal behaviour for a grown adult to lunch merrily on a piece of bread covered in sprinkles!

Step into any Dutch office cafeteria and you will find tiny boxes of sprinkles in different flavours being sold alongside the endless rows of bread and cheese. One can only giggle at the sight of a room of adult Dutch businessmen in striped shirts sipping on milk cartons and eating chocolate sprinkle sandwiches. Perhaps they didn't get the memo that they were in fact lunching on fairy toast (the UK term for the children's treat!)

Hagelslag comes in a few varieties, although chocolate is the staple. If you are looking to eat a bit healthier, why not opt instead for the fruit-flavoured variety?

To put all this sprinkle-eating madness into perspective, we will share with you a little-known fact: Dutch people consume over 14 million kilos of *hagelslag* each year. Yes, 14 million kilos! Do you know what that means? That's roughly the combined weight of 1000 adult elephants! (Aren't facts more fun when measured in elephants?)

Personally, we can do without these colourful sprinkle-ly meals, but if these sugar-filled morning treats bring a smile to a Dutch person's face, then we're all for it. Heck, what else is going to on a rainy Dutch winter day?

WHAT OUR COMMUNITY HAS TO SAY

I am first generation Canadian and grew up eating hagelslag on toast for breakfast. We would sometimes Canadian-ize it by first spreading peanut butter on the toast and then cover with hagelslag …. mmmmm

Jim

Growing up as a first generation American, I was forever teased about my "chocolate sandwiches" in grade school. It didn't help I was a tad on the chunky side either. However, they were delicious on white bread! Also on toast, which made the Hagelslag all melty. Yummm!!!

Karen

Germans have their own version: super thin chocolate bars or slices that are as big as half a slice of bread, you take two for a slice or one on a folded slice. Is great, more chocolate and less spilling over.

Joke

I have a tip for everyone going to the Netherlands: get some brown, wholewheat bread, smear a freaking thick layer of butter on it, preferably cold, and apply the darkest, most cacao-laden sprinkles on it, but not too much in proportion to the bread and butter (the 70%, smaller variety of De Ruijter is heavy stuff). THAT'S how you do chocolate sprinkles.

Crystal

Chocolate was considered the food of gods by the Incas and Maya's, so what's wrong with continuing that tradition? And don't even start comparing Chocolate Hagelslag to "sprinkles" you use on ice-cream. They don't even taste like chocolate.

Hagelslag actually means the sound of hail falling onto something (street, car caravan whatever) Also if your car gets dented from a hailstorm, those little dings are refered to by car mechanics and insurance companies alike as hagelslag. Come to think of it, when looking at a boterham met hagelslag it kinda sorta resembles a hailstorm (well, if you've drank enough beer that is).

Tom

I remember some of my old Dutch co-workers who always enjoy their hagelslag on bread lunch so much that they never want to spoil any leftover hagelslag on their plates. Yep, you got me right, they would pick those tiny little sweet stuff one by one with their finger and put them on their tounge to eat it, til the very last piece. I find it very disturbing yet amusing.

Nori

#4 DUTCH DIRECTNESS

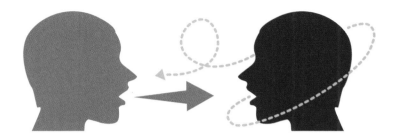

You've heard the rumours, the stereotypes and all the clichés - and we are here to tell you, that like the majority of gossip, they are, in fact... all absolutely true! Dutch people are direct. Direct to the point of shocking at times. Direct to the point of gasp! And direct to the point of *"what the f@#$ did he just say to me?!?* If you plan on spending any time in the Lowlands you had better get used to it, and fast!

This Dutch trait has gone by many names; call it what you will – abrupt, bad-mannered, barbaric, blunt, brusque, cheeky, crude, curt, direct, discourteous, forthright, frank, graceless, gruff, honest, ignorant, impolite, inconsiderate, insulting, intrusive, matter-of-fact, open, outspoken, plain, point-blank, raw, refreshing, rude, sincere, straightforward, surprising, uncouth or unmannerly. Essentially, the bottom line remains. The Dutch like to speak their minds.

We're not saying it's *necessarily* a bad thing. We're just telling you how it is. Dutch people don't mince words. You certainly won't find them biting their tongues or dying for that extra ounce of courage to finally speak freely. Don't feel like hearing from your co-worker that she actually doesn't think your new haircut is all that nice. Too bad. Don't want to know that the speech you just made and worried about might have sucked, did in fact suck, and big time!

Our advice... *Get used to it.* In the Netherlands you are very likely to hear a lot of statements that in other cultures politely fall into the category of "better left unsaid". Whereas nationalities such as the British, Canadian, Australian and in some cases American, shy away from discussing "hot topics" such as religion, immigration, politics and money, Dutch people revel in such lively and opinion-fuelled debate.

Dutch people value honesty and sincerity. What we (non-Dutch peeps) might consider rude or blunt, the Dutch perceive as honest and truthful. In fact they pride themselves in having and expressing an opinion.

The Dutch are in fact proud of this directness and their "unique" *tell-it-like-they-see-it* mentality. They often view American or British politeness as a sign of weakness reeking of insincerity and hypocrisy (two equally despised traits).

Not quite sure if you can handle Dutch directness? Well, in the words of the famously "direct" Dutch speed-skater Sven Kramer, *"Are you stupid?"* *

This was Kramer's televised response to a foreign journalist who dared to ask him his name at the Winter Olympics in 2010.

WHAT OUR COMMUNITY HAS TO SAY

Ah yes, directness. We've all been on the receiving end of this. At least you know where you stand!

Linda

Although I consider directness to be a good thing, it clears up things very fast you can be too direct. Some times it is very unnecessary to sa y certain things, the Netherlands that seem to think indeed that being rude is the same as being honest...to me it looks like those people are more frequent in the western part of the Netherlands especially the Rotterdam area. That's what I have experienced at least and I didn't like it.

Joop

Heusfoto

Being Dutch, 'directness' is not something we should be proud of. I'm not.

Acolade

I personally think that can go both ways. Yes, sometimes it's not cool to tell someone their speech sucked, and how/why it sucked. But if people keep saying it was a good speech the person in question might not know and never improve his speech-giving abilities. There is a difference between honesty and tactlessness though… Speak your mind but do it in a gentle way.

Mandy

OK, when it's an important subject, but does anyone really need to hear everyone's opinions on their haircut? If "speaking your mind" means hurting someone, or making them unhappy for no good reason, surely it's better to be kind. Most people's minds aren't so fantastic that we need to know what's in them every minute of the day.

Sylvia

I am from Rotterdam, I've lived here my entire life. We are more direct than people from other sides of the country. Others and definitely non-dutchies would call us rude. We're the kind that indeed would tell our friends: 'Yes, you do look fat in those pants, if I were you I would never put them on again! Ever!' My friends, family and I like it this way. We know what we all think of each other and there is indeed no big elephant in the room. We know we can ALWAYS count on each other and be honest to each other.

Dellai

Being Dutch and have been living abroad for a long time I fully agree with you. There is absolutely nothing wrong with being nice to each other, especially at an office with your colleagues. In the US they are so much more friendly and positive and when I adapted that behavior I felt better instantly. When you're friendly with others this will reflect to your personality too. I don't want to pick on service jobs but it's so much better when you are serviced in a nice polite way other than the Dutch rude "please f*ck off, I'm having a break" way.

Rochejagu

If you are direct and it hurts a person's feelings (and you know that) then that is being rude. Telling the truth requires some degree of tact and diplomacy.

17

It's not only negative, because you get the honest opinion and won't have to doubt. If something is great, you will also get a confirmation. Although some people are offended by it, it is a very efficient way of communication. It gets rid of frustration and stress.

Simon

I was proposed to by a Dutchman and he added 'but please do something about the weight'. Needless to say I told him where to go...

Sad Sally

Using their directness to be indirect is an art. They can give 'complimenten' to which you don't know whether to feel insulted or smile. How to say when a co-worker with a genuine smile in the face tells you "you can wear something pretty every once in a while, 'zeg'". hmmmm Thanks?

Diana

It's funny this directness, my husband, early on in our relationship, would feel slightly embarrassed at dinner parties where I would "revel" in exciting debates about religion, politics who to vote, why are you put on this planet & etc. (instead of the English topics such as cars, house prices, mortgages & council bin collection!!! Even after 11yrs of living in Britain it's still the same topics)! Also he felt that most of the time my family just argued when in fact we felt we were having a nice evening with a lively political debate. He over it now and we made him an honorary Dutch person!! I sometimes miss the directness and trying to figure out where you stand with people I feel, living in England, can be pretty tough. Since no-one is really like the Dutch.

Judith

The point of the article is not quite "the Dutch speak their minds" but more like "there is a thin line between speaking your mind and being a tactless asshole and the Dutch often like to get too close to it" (or at least, more often than in other cultures). Although, to my dismay, I have experience how certain Dutch people (of course, not a majority) who are proud of "being direct" (which often includes derogatory opinions about your country) can't handle "directness" in the opposite direction. Being a foreigner in this country I don't feel that this "Dutch directness" is such a big deal, it's just part of the "cultural divide". However it tends to create awkward moments and an impression of arrogant behavior.

Ignacio

Being direct is not the problem. Being rude is. A colleague of mine also had bad breath once, but was passing through my department on his way to his department. A coworker made a gesture behind his back just before we met. I obviously noticed what the gesture meant when he got closer and greeted me. I took him aside and told him he had very bad breath. I did not expect him to get angry because I wanted to shield him from a lot of gossip. His face turned red not from anger but from shame, after which he couldn't thank me enough for pointing it out to him. He just wasn't aware. I gave him a roll of peppermints and called him in sick. He went to the dentist straight away. Problem solved, no gossip, friends forever.Now I would like to know how a British colleague would have let him take the fall.

Cloggy

As a Dutchy living in rural England, I cannot tell you how much I miss our directness since I always have to guess what people really mean here.

Thea

Finally! Someone wrote it down:-)))BEDANKT! It's sooooo, soooo true! and it's very disturbing for all other, non-Dutch persons...although after 7 years here I start to realize that it is somehow contagious...grrr!

Jana

During my visit to Holland to finalize the expat agreement, my new boss invited me to his house for dinner. We walk in, I greet a 9 year old son who loudly states "wow, hij is dik." Quite embarrassed, the new boss tried to overlook the statement. I pulled it out of him and was told that "I was fat." Being true, I agreed. I now have a favorite sentence in Dutch, "Ik ben dik, maar slim."

Tim

I've come across the directness thing when living in different countries and however hard I try to strike the right balance between politeness, saving face and conveying my honest opinion to those who are important to me. I still tend to end up on the too direct end of the scale. My parents always told me: "you might not like to hear this, but at least we'll be honest with you." So to me, directness to the point of rudeness is a true sign of love and caring.

Katrijn

19

When i moved to Canada 20 years ago, I was told that I was rude and too direct. However I adjusted. I learned a lot from living with so many cultures around me. Canada is a land of immigrants and people respect each other. Now I'm back in the Netherlands and I get upset about that Dutch, right in your face, rudeness. Dutch people push their opinion right through your throat. I prefer the Canadian Politeness above the Dutch, often, disrespectful rudeness. When there is a chance, I'll move back.

Wilma

Being subtle, modest and humble is just not in my dictionary. Wasn't raised like that. Never my intention to hurt anybody, on the contrary, I feel that honesty makes me connect on a deeper level with other people. Cut the crap, get real.

Chrissie

I am Dutch. I was travelling in the US and had lunch with our representatives, US citizens. This big guy was piling up his plate from the salad bar, using about everything that was there: Mushrooms, bacon, eggs, salad, tomato, etc.etc. He finished it eating with one hand (disgusting) and redid the whole ritual again. Drank enormous cups of coffee with it; then he went for the Kings cut of Prime rib, a one inch thick piece of meat that covered the whole plate, with side servings of French Fries and vegetables. Coffee and ice water. He gobbled it up, finishing his plate earlier than the other guys at the table. I told him: You are going to see the doctor soon! He asked me why. I said: He will build a second ass-hole for you, there is no way that this one ass-hole of yours will be able to handle that amount of processed food much longer. He told me: That's rude Peter.

Peter

I guess that is rude Peter but on the other hand, caring. Someone has to wake up an irresponsible lifestyle.

DTP District

#5 BATTLING WATER

Many think of The Netherlands as a passive, peaceful country, but let it be known that Dutch people have a mortal enemy; an adversary with whom they have fought with for centuries. Whether it originated from sheer determination, ingenuity, necessity or foolishness, no other nation has waged war on water - and won, quite like the Dutch.

The war on water has been a tough one and not without casualties; the great flood of 1953 killed over 1,800 people and wiped out 2 entire villages. Dutch people, however, have amassed many a victory along the way. They hold the title for reclaiming the largest piece of land in the world – the "*Flevopolder*" (the word "polder" refers to low-lying land reclaimed using a system of drainage dikes). They can also claim the title for the world's largest artificial island.

So who does one of the richest countries in the world call when they want to make some fancy islands in the middle of the Persian Gulf? The Dutch of course! The Palm Islands project in Dubai was headed by the Dutch company, *Van Oord* who, not surprisingly, specialises in land reclamation and has been in business since the early 1800s.

Astoundingly, one sixth of the Netherlands (7000 km²) is actually reclaimed land. Stranger yet, 60% of Dutch people now live below sea level - it turns out that even their enormous height can't help them in this case!

If evolution worked like a sci-fi film, modern-day Dutch would be born with fish-like gills and webbed feet. How handy!

Instilled in the very DNA of a Dutch person is the primal desire to battle the elements. With a 2000 year history of reclaiming land from the sea, one can only agree that, "God created the world, but the Dutch created Holland".

WHAT OUR COMMUNITY HAS TO SAY

The Dutch also used water as a way to defend the country, it is known as "De Hollandse Waterlinie".

Wesley

I like that concept of just flooding your polders if the enemy is near to protect your cities...

Henk

BTW ...our new King's previous job was "water manager", just to illustrate that it's imbedded in all layers of our society.

Dutch

I'm American and when I was visiting Amsterdam a few years back some Dutch guys overheard me discussing New Orleans and the hurricane in a bar. They came up to our table and were like "Why doesn't the US just hire some Dutchies already to fix New Orleans problem?! We could have helped big time, we've been fighting with water for centuries and we're winning!". We all drank to that!!

Dylan

God created the world, but the Dutch created Holland!!!

Marieke

Ummm. No. People created God.

Kevin

...and God said (to the DUTCH), "WELL DONE "!!!!

Tom

#6 THREE KISSES

You may have noticed that Dutch people are a rather kissy bunch. Plop yourself down on any terrace in town and take in the sight of Dutch people all around you greeting & kissing & kissing & kissing! An odd practice for a normally rather reserved bunch. What is all this kissing about? Who exactly kisses who, and more importantly, when is the right moment for all this kissing?

We at SDPL are here to make the mysteries of the Lowlands a little less mysterious. Kissing is indeed a rather important cultural norm in the Netherlands. However, social kissing does come with its own precise set of rules and regulations:

1. It is common practice to greet people with kisses.

2. Kisses, however, are not indiscriminately doled out to just anyone; they are strictly reserved for friends and relatives only*.

3. The norm these days is three kisses on the cheek.

4. These kisses however are not actual kisses on the cheek; they are more like air-kisses and your moist lips should not actually touch the other person.

5. The three air-kisses are used to greet someone and also to say goodbye.

6. Women are all about the kissing: women kiss women and women kiss men.

7. Men generally only kiss women (apart from their relatives).

8. Men greet each other instead with a very manly and firm handshake.

9. Kissing follows the pattern right cheek – left cheek – right cheek; don't dare go rogue or you are sure to cause a face-on collision.

10. Work is not a place for kissing, unless it is someone's birthday or the start of a new year.

*The infamous "three kisses" are not exchanged with friends or family whom you see on a daily basis. For example, you would only greet friends with kisses if you hadn't seen them for some time.

Confused much?! Who would've thought that a simple little greeting could have such a complicated set of rules? Of course, there are always awkward moments and situations that even our handy 10-step rules can't solve. *What if you go a little too enthusiastically into a kiss and painfully smack cheek bones, do you then give an apology kiss? More importantly, when is the right moment to wipe someone's sweat/spit off your face after a rather moist encounter?*

VERY CHEEKY
A quick guide to greetings in the Netherlands

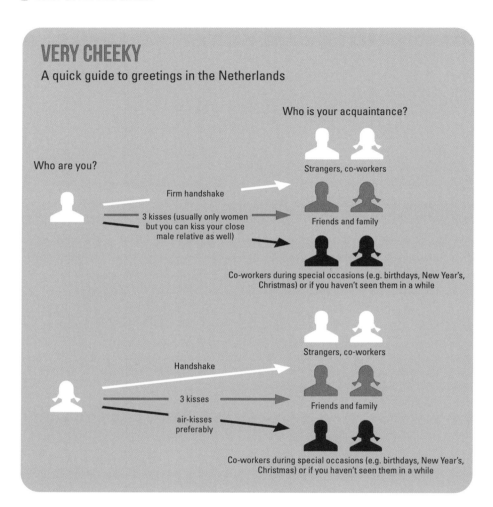

Who is your acquaintance?

Strangers, co-workers

Who are you?

Firm handshake

3 kisses (usually only women but you can kiss your close male relative as well)

Friends and family

Co-workers during special occasions (e.g. birthdays, New Year's, Christmas) or if you haven't seen them in a while

Strangers, co-workers

Handshake

3 kisses

Friends and family

air-kisses preferably

Co-workers during special occasions (e.g. birthdays, New Year's, Christmas) or if you haven't seen them in a while

WHAT OUR COMMUNITY HAS TO SAY

Hem hem hem…there is a silent war between in-the-air-kissersand the rest of us good, honest, non-fake-ass people who *will* actually kiss you, however, no saliva is allowed, as is more than a very slight moistness of the lips. Occasionally a runny nose can't be avoided and is generally forgiven.

Densetsu Shun

Don't forget the confusion between the people who kiss twice and those who kiss thrice. Always an awkward moment if u go in for the third one when the other pulled out early.

Jeroen

Pulling out early is always a little awkward!

John

Two men, when relatives, or very close friends, do in fact kiss as part of the greeting. It always gets looks when I pick up my dad or brother from the airport in the U.S.

Mark

Interesting trivia to know: the three kisses actually mean something. It means (as far as I remember), a kiss for you, a kiss for me and a kiss for the queen.

Great site, laughing at my own oddities, being dutch.

Jeroen

I'm originally from the south of the Netherlands (born in Limburg, raised in Noord Brabant), and to me three kisses were very normal throughout the 1960/70s. But then, when I started studying in Utrecht and later in Amsterdam, I noticed it wasn't a common custome there at all. And indeed I was told, it was something that only people from the south would do. Well, it's spread almost everywhere by now, it seems, though I'm not sure about Friesland and Groningen..

Arthur

While heterosexual men usually don't kiss other male non-relatives, I have seen Dutch gay men do the three-kiss-greeting with other gay men who were only acquaintances.

Michael

27

#7 ORANGE

Perhaps you've noticed that Dutch people like the colour orange. Look around and you will start to notice that the love of orange is all around you. It's even available as sprinkles for your toast. It doesn't take a rocket scientist to realise that the Netherlands' unofficial national colour is orange.

Why orange? After all, the Dutch flag is red, white and blue. Well, dear readers, don't believe everything you see - the original colours of the Dutch flag were in fact, orange, white and blue!

A short look back in history can explain more. Once upon a time, there was a young boy called *Willem van Oranje* who was born into nobility in 1533. Willem became the *Prince of Orange* in 1544 and lead the Dutch revolt against the

Spanish, eventually resulting in the formal independence of the United Provinces in 1648. This Willem character was needless to say, rather important and is fondly referred to as the *father of the fatherland*. The colours of the national flag thus represented him (and the *House of Orange*). He was forever idolised in the Dutch national anthem (translated for your reading pleasure):

William of Nassau,
Am I, of German descent*
Loyal to the fatherland
I will remain until I die
A Prince of Orange
Am I, free and fearless
The king of Spain
I have always honoured

*The mention of German blood will incite quite the heated debate amongst Dutchies, although this is indeed the literal translation.

The Orange bloodline thrived and grew throughout the ages and in 1815, after a long period as a republic, the Netherlands became a monarchy (as it remains today) under the House of Orange-Nassau.

There are many hypotheses as to why the orange in the Dutch flag was eventually changed to red:
· a national shortage of orange dye
· sailors could not adequately see the orange flag from a distance
· the colour faded to yellow too often in the sun
· the house of Orange simply lost its popularity

No theory has actually been proven, but it is known that red replaced the orange at the end of the 80 years war in 1648.

You may have noticed that Dutch people get out their orange gear *en masse* at least once a year to celebrate King's day. Orange garb also makes an appearance at sporting events. *Oranje* can in fact refer to many things: the royal family, the national football team, or the colour itself. Confused? When in doubt, just wear orange.

WHAT OUR COMMUNITY HAS TO SAY

First of all, love your blog it's really a refreshing read for a Dutchman. I think the translation "Ben ik van Duitsen bloed" into "Am I, of German descent" is incorrect and only furthers the confusion some have with distinguishing between the Dutch and the German who speak Deutsch.
"Duitsen", in the time it was written meant, a whole different place than what is now known as Germany. "Duitsland" could be roughly translated to "of the people". Seeing that I'm not a historian I will not try to reproduce my wikipedia-found knowledge. As far as I can tell "van Duitsen bloed" refers to "de 17 provinciën" which later seperated into Dietsland (The Netherlands and Flanders) and Deutschland (Germany).

Raoul

Actually, the people who say that 'Duitschen' means Dutch instead of German are wrong, it does mean German. Why? Because the anthem is about Wilhelmus van Nassau, who was born in what is Germany and because back then, there really wasn't much of a difference between Dutch and German. For some reason my fellow Dutchmen like to twist and forget our own history; Our language comes from German, we were under German rule and were exactly the same as the Germans for ages, Wilhelmus was German, and even our royal family in these times is full of German blood (Prins Bernhard and Prins Claus). Almost every Dutch person has German ancestry. We have always had extremely good relations with the Germans and Germany until Hitler ruined it, but now the more unintelligent Dutch people hate Germany just because they don't understand their own ancestry and history.

Een Nederlander

Our language does not come from German. It is a Germanic language, just like German. There is a difference there.And I also disagree on your last statement, I don't think people still hate the Germans. It's more like a sibling kind of thing, where we kind of tease each other (I always thought it was a one way thing, but since I moved to Germany, I found out they have quite a lot of jokes about us as well), but without any actual harm intended. Sort of like what we have with Belgium, but then with us Dutchies in the role of the smaller, younger sibling.

Sytske

Although we may come across as slightly crazy wearing so much orange, we are always happy and everyone is welcome to join in (tourist always say everyone is very jovial on Queen's Day).

Well, I think in the Netherlands, it is such a distinctive color, i.e. always associated with a special event, that if you wear it on a day that there is no event, that it looks kinda silly .But also, orange is not a very flattering color on pale people so I guess that's why we don't wear it regularly. Cause when you're drunk, everyone looks great. Even pale people in orange.

I think in fact that dutch people hate orange.. you'll never see anyone wear orange besides events like queens day or football matches.

Anna

Geraldine

#8 NOT OWNING CURTAINS

Dutch people like living a curtain-less existence, thereby showing the world they have nothing to hide. Take a leisurely stroll down any Dutch street and you are sure to notice one startling similarity, a persistent lack of drawn curtains and hence, no personal privacy. We do have to admit that our voyeuristic tendencies are heartily fulfilled in Amsterdam!

Curious about the neighbour's décor or sense of style? Want to know what *Jaap* and his family are eating for dinner? Want to know what most Dutch folks are watching on their *televisie* in the evenings? Luckily, you can find the answers to all your questions (and much, much more) behind Dutch people's naked, street-level apartment windows.

Of course, some Dutch do in fact own curtains, but they too join in the fun by having their curtains proudly drawn allowing the contents of their abodes to be proudly shown. They seem to get as much entertainment (or perhaps even more) looking out and observing who is looking in. It makes you wonder which side of the aquarium you are standing on.

MY FAVOURITE JAUNT AROUND MY NEIGHBOURHOOD LEADS ME PAST WHAT I LIKE TO REFER TO AS MY DUTCH BUNDY FAMILY (MARRIED WITH CHILDREN). ON A TYPICAL EVENING, THE WHOLE FAMILY CAN BE SEEN SQUEEZED INTO THEIR TINY LIVING ROOM WATCHING SOME POPULAR DUTCH TV SHOW. YOU SEE VADER WEARING NOTHING BUT HIS LEOPARD-PRINT UNDERWEAR. MOEDER AND DOCHTER COIFFED WITH THE SAME SPIKEY RED MULLETS, ALONG WITH ZOON AND HOND ALL SQUISHED ONTO THEIR PURPLE VELOUR COUCH MUNCHING ON SNACKS.

I HAVE TO ADMIT THAT EVERY TIME I WALK BY THEIR HOUSE I CAN'T HELP BUT STARE. IT'S LIKE A BAD CAR ACCIDENT AND I AM STUCK, LIKE A DEER IN HEADLIGHTS, UNABLE TO LOOK AWAY!

Much has been discussed about this matter. The common consensus is that it stems from Dutch people's Calvinistic roots, because allowing passersby a full view of your living quarters shows you have nothing to hide.

Our theory on the matter is slightly different and has nothing to do with Calvinism. The answer is much more simplistic and can be summed up in 5 letters: L-I-G-H-T. Dutch people love the sun and quite frankly, many of their ground-floor and *souterrain* (basement) apartments are nothing more than dark, sombre dungeons.

Without the curtains open and the light pouring in, Dutch people would essentially live like underground moles for most of the year, travelling from dark apartment, to dark outside, to dark workplace with a possible stop-over at a dark brown cafe and then back to said dark apartment. Leaving the curtains open is essentially a basic human survival technique, a meagre attempt at fighting the never-ending Dutch battle of Vitamin D deficiency.

WHAT OUR COMMUNITY HAS TO SAY

My husband's family is frisian and when we visited I noticed they (at least) like to put little doo-dads and thing-a-ma-gigs in on the window sill to show to the passersby. Everyone does it. If you had curtains you wouldn't be able to show the world your latest acquisition for your window sill.

Mandy

I think that part of the reason some Dutch people like the fact that others can look in their homes, is to show how clean and gezellig it is and how all the silver and brass is polished and how nice the clock is! ha!

Maria

I grew up walking the dog through the neighborhood at night and a big part of the enjoyment was looking into everyone's living room while passing by. Last time I was there I noticed they all have these plastic strips glued to the windows so I guess looking in is not done anymore. I will miss it.

Rightie

I'm a Dutchie myself, and believe me, I do own curtains and I use them!

Carolien

You seriously couldn't be more right! I work for a couple and clean their house, the male from Scotland and the woman from Estland, they always have the curtains and shutters closed! So when I come by I first open them all and let the bleak winter light in. I think bleak winter light is always better than electric light.
~ A very Dutch student

Judith

Why bother with curtains? They need cleaning (especially if dad in his leopard skin undies smokes), and they take all the fun away for people on the street. Besides, not having curtains is good for the consumption of energy. Why pay for illumination if you already pay taxes that the city uses to illuminate the streets. Curtains are for people with money to spend.

sven

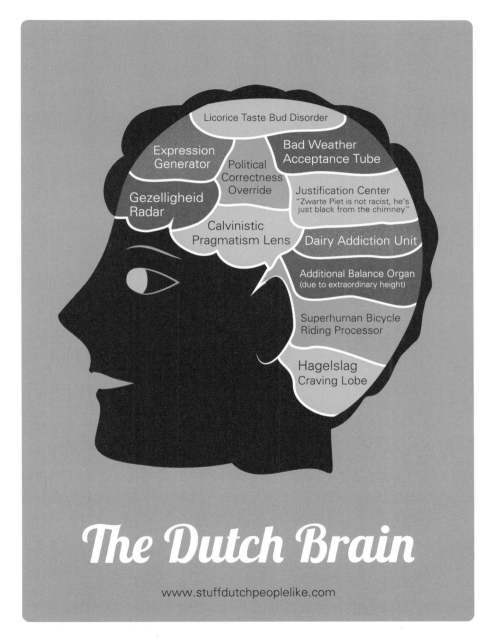

The Dutch Brain

www.stuffdutchpeoplelike.com

#9 TULIPS

When most people think of the Dutch, they think of windmills, clogs and tulips. All very Dutch indeed – apart from the tulip that is. This precious symbol of the Netherlands is in fact not really Dutch in origin!

The tulip's colourful presence in the Netherlands is owed to the Ottoman Empire (by way of trade) and later, a Flemish botanist who discovered that the unusual flowers thrived in the harsh climate of the Lowlands.

Tulips and the Dutch have an illustrious and chequered past good enough for the history books. Although incomprehensible, at the height of their Golden Age popularity one measly tulip bulb could fetch 10 times the annual salary of a skilled worker (or as much as one of Amsterdam's prestigious canal houses).

The Dutchies were simply mad for those little bulbs! So mad in fact, that in 1637 their irrational enthusiasm for the flowers triggered a speculative frenzy and a subsequent spectacular market crash. Many a Dutchie lost their entire life's savings (and apparently their minds) in what came to be known as *Tulipmania*.

Modern day economists love to refer to *Tulipmania* as the first-ever stock market crash. Only the burst of the dot-com bubble (in 2000) and the American housing market crisis (in 2008) come close to the ramifications of the infamous *Tulipmania*.

The market did eventually recover although the good old days of the golden era did come to an end. The crash, however, only temporarily dampened the Dutch's passion for tulips and they took to the flower trade like bees to honey. Dutch flower exports now make up a 5 billion euro industry and chances are the tulips (or any other flower for that matter) you gave your sweetheart last week in New York (to make up for being such a grouchy bore) were in fact born and bred on Dutch soil.

WHAT OUR COMMUNITY HAS TO SAY

Supposedly, the first Dutchman who received a tulip bulb as a gift did not know what it was or what to do with it, so he had his staff prepare it for a meal...

Ginandtonic

I ate cookies made from ground up tulip bulbs. . . during WW2!

Lieke

Well, yes. We're not really inventers. We do sales a LOT better!

Dutch

"...chances are the tulips you gave your sweetheart last week in New York to make up for being such a grouchy bore were in fact born and bred on Dutch soil!" Or any other flower for that matter!"

Derk

The Dutch don't invent, they just sell you your own stuff.Like my Oma said: "Jongen, if we could sell our mother we'd do it. But the price needs to be right.

Irving

How ironic. We Turkish now buy our tulips from the Dutch!

Mehmet

(#10) BIRTHDAY CONGRATULATIONS

I'VE NEVER BEEN SO CONFUSED IN MY LIFE, AS WHEN I FIRST ATTENDED THE BIRTHDAY PARTY OF A DUTCH FRIEND. I HAD LIVED IN THE NETHERLANDS A LITTLE UNDER A YEAR, AND IT HAPPENED TO BE MY FIRST REAL DUTCH SOCIAL AFFAIR. I ARRIVED AT THE PARTY AND WITHIN MINUTES HAPPENED TO BE ON DOOR-DUTY. A GROUP OF THE BIRTHDAY BOY'S FRIENDS WALKED IN AND IMMEDIATELY GAVE ME 3 SMOOCHY AIR-KISSES FOLLOWED BY A TRIO OF ENTHUSIASTIC "CONGRATULATIONS!" I SMILED AWKWARDLY. THAT WAS ODD! CONGRATULATIONS FOR WHAT? I SCANNED MY MIND FOR A LIST OF RECENT ACCOMPLISHMENTS... AH HA – THE JOB PROMOTION! I DIDN'T REALIZE THEY KNEW? ...NICE OF THEM TO CONGRATULATE ME ON IT, I SUPPOSED.

AFTER MOVING INTO THE LIVING ROOM, I WAS GREETED BY MY FRIEND'S MOTHER AND SHE AGAIN CONGRATULATED ME, THIS TIME WITH A THROATY DUTCH "GEFELICITEERD"! I MUTTERED A QUICK "OH, IT'S REALLY NOT A BIG DEAL..." WHICH GARNERED QUITE AN ODD LOOK FROM HER BEFORE MOVING ON. WHAT HAPPENED NEXT WAS COMPLETELY UNEXPECTED: THE ENTIRE ROOM SUDDENLY ERUPTED INTO A FLURRY OF "GEFELICITEERD"S. EVERYBODY WAS SUDDENLY BUSY CONGRATULATING SOMEONE ELSE. WHAT THE HECK WAS GOING ON? WAS THERE A GROUP LOTTERY WIN I DIDN'T KNOW ABOUT?!

To adequately navigate a Dutch birthday you will need to:

1.   Congratulate the person whose birthday it is. This sounds simple but you will need to use the Dutch word *gefeliciteerd* which requires first mastering the Dutch "g", so start practicing!

2. Make your way around the circle of seated guests and congratulate everyone who is close to the person whose birthday it is. This means congratulating their mother, father wife, husband, *oma, opa,* the cat, the dog - you name it!

3. Dole out three kisses, where appropriate

4. Eat one piece of cake and be merry!

Needless to say, you may have caught on that Dutch people like congratulating each other on their birthdays. When hanging around this lanky bunch, you will also need to congratulate the person whose birthday it is. Of course offering congratulations seems a little over the top for us non-Dutchies, as in English the term is most often reserved for big occasions such as weddings and births. An annual birthday just doesn't seem to merit such fanfare.

But, what exactly are you congratulating people for? Congratulations on being born? Congratulations on surviving another year? The whole thing is beyond confusing.

One thing's for sure, while living in the Lowlands you will get an awful lot of congratulations. A hell of a lot more than in other countries. In fact, it will almost feel like your own birthday on other people's big day!

WHAT OUR COMMUNITY HAS TO SAY

Must leave many 'non' Dutch people confused. I always love it when people call and congratulate me with either my hubby's birthday or the birthdays of my children." Other-landers" are just missing out!

Smit

I completely agree with this description of a birthday party. When I go to a family party, it feels like you are in a receiving line at a wedding, because you must congratulate them, shake their hand and also kiss three times. I know of fathers and mothers who congratulate each other on their child's birthday. I have only been here 7 months, but I have heard the word congratulate more in these past months then ever in my whole life. Hey, if the Dutch are happy and it makes them smile, it is a good thing.

Jane

Haha, awesome read! As a Dutch person I have a theory about why this happens. I think, people who are close to the birthday party-host, get congratulations because they are in the "very close" social group. The people who are close to each other help and take care of each other. So I think it makes sense to congratulate the close friends and familie because they helped get the "jarige" get through a whole year. Saying "en gefeliciteerd to all of you" is actually sending the message that you don't know who are the close people to the birthdayboy. I think... maybe I've never really thought about it.my two cents

Roy

This probably started when someone was at a birthday party and did not know who's birthday it was. So he congratulated everyone, that way you are sure you did congratulate the one.I'm from spain, i refuse to congratulate everyone. I will kiss the good looking ones, as in spain we do dish out a lot of kisses to family and friends. So the trick to a international traveler, combine what you like forget the rest:-)

Jordi

When I congratulated my Canadian boyfriend on his best friend's birthday he was very confused too! I explained to him and he answered: "That's another weird thing you can put on the list."We Dutch people are quite weird if you think about it!

Maggie

41

Joanny

One time, before I knew this was a typical Dutch thing to do, I was in the UK and went to a friend's (note: he's British and this was the first time meeting his friends and family) birthday and I was already late and embarrassed about that so I congratulated everyone and excused myself for being late then rushed to the toilet.. When I came back everyone was staring at me and finally his dad asked me why I did that so I said "because its your sons birthday" with the most awkward grin on my face, my friend took me aside to tell me how he forgot to tell me that they don't do that, so after I explained how normal it is here it kinda became the joke of the night haha.

Jos

'Congratulating' everybody on a birthday party is indeed quite common in the Netherlands. However outlanders shouldn't translate it as 'congratulations', but more as a standard greeting. In the Netherlands it's more usual to say 'Gefeliciteerd' instead of 'Hallo' which is the normal greeting for casual meetings. But if you say 'Hallo' to everyone on a birthday party it sounds rather boring, so most people prefer to say 'Gefeliciteerd' as a greeting. So in the Dutch it's quite normal to greet everyone on a birthday party when you arrive. Is that also typically Dutch? I think it's a good social behaviour. Also, when there is someone at the party you don't know, you say: 'Gefeliciteerd, (ik ben) Jos'. So it's actually also a way to introducing yourself to people at the party you don't know. That's in my opinion the main reason why Dutch people do this. It will avoid situations at the party when you are talking in a group and don't know each others names, which I personally find pretty awkward.

Ron

Although I'm Dutch, I never knew about this custom until I moved from the south of Limburg to Utrecht. I still find it absurdly odd to congratulate everyone with the birthday just because they were invited to the party.Perhaps that's the reason: they congratulate each other on getting another free piece of cake! We're Dutch, after all .

#11 DISCUSSING THE WEATHER

Dutch people love to discuss the weather. Want to join in a friendly chat with your Dutch co-workers or neighbours? Not sure what exactly they are discussing intensely by the *Douwe Egberts* machine? Chances are it's the fascinating and captivating topic of the weather!

Is your Dutch a bit rusty? Just throw in a *"Mooi weertje, he?"* (Nice weather, eh?) or a dramatic *"Wat een hondeweer!"* (What shite weather!) and it is sure to lead into a (semi-) friendly chat with a stranger.

Dutch people are highly in tune with the imminent and future weather conditions. Will it rain this afternoon? Need a 4-day forecast? Chances are any Dutch person in your vicinity will have a very accurate weather prediction for you. Actually there is no need for trained meteorologists in the

. . . . **WEATHER FACTS**
AMSTERDAM

AVERAGE HUMIDITY 82.5%

215 RAINY DAYS /YEAR

#4 EUROPE'S RAINIEST CITY

Netherlands as the Dutch spend so much time discussing and tracking the weather that they practically all have honorary degrees in the subject!

Technology has allowed Dutch people to move even further ahead in the war on weather. It's no surprise that one of the most popular iPhone apps in Holland is *Buienradar* – a weather tracking system showing you the exact time it will rain and for precisely how long. Word of warning: *Buienradar* is downright addictive. Once you start tracking those looming grey clouds it will become progressively more difficult to plan your day (and your morning cycle to work) without compulsively checking the current precipitation status.

Dutch weather can also be used to predict the collective Dutch mood. If it's been rainy and grey outside for more than a few days the chances are that the Dutch are feeling a bit down and cranky. Is the sun shining? You bet the Dutch will be practically singing on every street corner (ok, that might be a big stretch for this socially reserved bunch, but you get the idea!)

Of course with all the water continually being dumped on this little country Dutch people have learned to prepare for the rain like no other nation. Sophisticated rain ponchos that hook onto your bicycle handlebars (cleverly allowing for dry hands while cycling), designer windproof umbrellas, and flashy rain pants are all part of normal daily gear.

On average there are 90 minutes of rain per day in the Netherlands. Call us a veritable genius, but we'd count on getting a bit wet every day of the year in this country. No need for fancy technology to tell you that!

WHAT OUR COMMUNITY HAS TO SAY

John R
This is something encountered quite often among sea-faring cultures, especially bordering unpredictable and potentially dangerous waters such as the North Sea. Keeping a close eye on the weather can pay off for fishermen if they can identify potentially harmful weather changes timely enough to make it back to port.

Tara
Hey! Don't bash the weather. Without it how would 99% of Dutch people start conversations.

Danny
John R hits the mark on this one I recon. The Dutch were and still are a nation of farmers, fisherman and sea-faring traders. Knowledge about the weather was priceless and it seems to have found a special place in the minds of the dutch people and it's almost impossible to count the number of Dutch expressions about the weather. (morgenrood is water in sloot, etc.) I know I'm guilty.

Mathijs
We'd still have "the weekend" to talk about. "Any plans for the weekend?" "How was your weekend?" and so on...

Stacey
This is so true! My colleagues are constantly checking their phones to see when the rain will start...and stop. They plan their days (and when to cycle to meetings) based on that app! Even my boss will be like "We have to leave now, because there is only a 15minute window before it starts raining!" hahaha

45

#12 LEKKER

If you've lived, toured, visited, or spent any amount of time in the Lowlands and you haven't heard this word we suggest you get your ears checked – and quick! This seemingly innocent word is ubiquitous in the Netherlands. Do a little good old fashioned eavesdropping in town (*if you haven't already*) and you are sure to hear multitudes of the "L" word.

lekker - / adjective /
nice
dainty
tasty
delicious
yummy
luscious
snug
tempting
enticing

Lekker in its original form refers to food and can be roughly translated into tasty or yummy. The Germans and Belgians use lekker this way. However, over time Dutch people have taken incredible liberties with the word and now essentially use it to describe, well, just about everything! A warm meal on a cold autumn day can of course be lekker, but so can a feeling, an experience, a place and even a person!

Word of warning: don't go around calling your co-workers or boss *lekker* as the original translation of yummy or tasty still applies!

(Of course, the tall Dutch boy in his red pants and gelled hair walking down the street may indeed be *lekker,* but shout that out to him at your own discretion!)

Lekker is a highly versatile little word and Dutch people use it in endless instances.

You will see that the original translation does not always hold true:

Expression	Literal translation	Actual meaning
Lekkere broodjes	Tasty sandwiches	Tasty sandwiches
Lekker rustig	Yummy calm	Pleasantly calm
Lekker weer	Tasty weather	Great weather
Niet lekker	Not yummy	Not nice, not well
Slaap lekker	Sleep tasty	Sleep tight, sleep well
Lekker ruim	Tasty space	Lots of space/room

Just to make things even more fun, Dutch people have mischievously paired one difficult-to-translate-word with yet another even-more-difficult-to -translate-word. The combination? The beautifully descriptive: *lekker gezellig!* Trust us, it does come in handy but we'll let you try to decipher the exact translation yourself!

EVER SEEN A DUTCH PERSON WAVING THEIR HAND MADLY AROUND THEIR EAR WHILE EATING? NO, IT'S NOT A NATIONAL TIC - IT'S THE NON-VERBAL SIGN FOR THE WORD "LEKKER"! GO AHEAD, GIVE IT A TRY!

WHAT OUR COMMUNITY HAS TO SAY

My American in laws always think I talk about 'liquor' instead of lekker, haha!

Chantal

Irritatingly ubiquitous. Like the way Americans use 'like' 10 times in every bloody sentence.

Steve

Love the word 'lekker – I taught my Aussie husband the word early on and he liked it so much he gave me personalised number plates with 'LEKKER'. Not just Dutchies but also people from South Africa and Zimbabwe have stopped/waved/commented when I drive around or am parked somewhere. And yeah, it comes from 'lekker ding' but that was too long…

Monique

I've had trouble explaining "lekker" to my American friends in the past "Lekker" can mean "comfortable". So "lekker druk" means "comfortably busy", which, if said in a happy / upbeat way, could mean the person is only slightly busy, but if it's said in a sarcastic / tired / exasperated voice, it means too busy

Gertjan

The worst use of the word "lekker" I've ever heard is "Ah, dat was lekker!" Sounds innocent, but to me, an "import-Dutchie" from Germany who associates "lekker" with "yummy", this is NOT wat you are expected to hear when your husband leaves the toilet after having a nice sh….!" LOL

Queen K

Don't forget to wave your hand around your ear when "lekkering"

Maija

I'm Dutch but living in Italy so your columns take me back home for a moment…And you're so right we really use the word Lekker for ANYthing…never realized it, but this post and comments really point it out. Ach, het is zo lekker Hollands

Dutchgoesitalian

SCHEDULING APPOINTMENTS

Spontaneity is not a strong point for Dutch people. Yes, they might like the 'concept' or 'idea' of spontaneity, but they usually have a hard time putting it into practice. In the Lowlands the concept of 'popping by' a friend's house just doesn't exit. *What, show up out of the blue? Without an appointment? Dat kan niet!*

Many a non-Dutch will be shocked by the constant sight of Dutch people pulling out their agendas (or iPhones) when planning a get-together. The more Dutchies you add to the mix, the more complicated the appointment-setting game gets. *Let's see, I am available in 3 weeks, but Fokke is only available the following week and Marieke can only do Wednesdays. So, it looks like it's a date in 6.5 weeks!*

You can try to fight this cultural phenomena, but if you spend time in the Lowlands the *ever-present-agenda-scheduling-addiction* will rub off on you. Believe it or not, many a Dutch person will even schedule "down-time" in their agendas *(e.g. December 3rd: Night on the couch!).*

A Dutch colleague once proudly announced that she had completely gotten rid of her agenda! She had reached her breaking point when scheduling dinner with her best friend, and discovered that the only date available in either of their agendas was in 4 months' time! She said that she had decided to live her life more spontaneously. The other Dutch colleagues around the table were incredulous! *"How do you plan on seeing anyone? How will you keep track of your appointments? Sorry, but that will never work!"*

After a few minutes of proudly reciting the virtues of an agenda-free-life, she looked down at the table and quietly mumbled, *"I'll admit it has been a bit hard to be spontaneous when everyone else is unavailable due to their fully booked agendas".* We're willing to bet that she fished that agenda out of the garbage in no time and was soon back on scheduled time! After all, it's hard work for a Dutchie to swim upstream – the orange current is very strong!

WHAT OUR COMMUNITY HAS TO SAY

This must be a real Northern thing then. I'm from the south of Holland, and it's more like opposite of that. Friends and family pop in all the time, without notice. If you're home, you're home, if you're not, they'll move on. Maybe people where you are have to cover bigger distances?

Bart

I doubt it is specifically a Northern thing. I lived for over 30 years in Breda until October 2008 and I hated it if people showed up without announcing, and not just me, everyone I knew had the same thing.

Jeroen

ahahahah I already got an agenda from my Dutch manager! Two months in Nederland and already getting integrated!

Simone

Your blog is just amazing, really funny and totally true. I'm totally Dutch and I think it's pretty normal to schedule everything. Why not? Yeah, sometimes I'm spontaneous, but most of the time I'm not. And I schedule 'me time' in my agenda.

Sarah

It's so true! I had a hissy fit when we were trying to "book in" for dinner with friends. A month in advance? Sorry, I'm not booking a dinner with friends a month in advance. Nobody is that busy.
I'd love to hear how the colleague sans agenda is coping, btw. I also reckon she's back to the agenda!

MissNeriss

As a non-Dutch person, and the idea of planners being totally foreign to me until I moved here, I can assure you that the rest of the world does just fine without them. We can indeed remember things without them. We're not always late and missing appointments.

Stingo

Haha, I am really dutch and i totally hate the whole agenda thing. But you really cannot escape from it. Love to read your blog. It's like a mirror. Thing we take for granted seen through the eyes of a non-dutch person. I love it!

Desi

This is one of the main reasons why I moved away from the Netherlands after living there for two and a half years. The lack of spontaneity and the "I will see you again in three month's time at 7:25 PM" just made me run away. I once called a friend with an urgent, life-or-death problem and I asked if I could see him and he told me (it was on a Tuesday), I kid you not, "Let me get my agenda… How's Saturday morning for you?" Most Dutch people I talked to about this never understood my shock…

Manja

Pulling our agenda's and making the appointment right on the spot is more an act of following through than of lack of spontaneity, if you ask me. I've been living in the US for 16 years now and it still bugs me when ppl say: let's get together for dinner (and it never happens if I don't pull my calendar and say: let's get it on the calendar then!). I love spontaneity, even before I left Holland.

Coach

Although the agenda-setting may seem excessive, the efficiency might be the reason the Dutch work the least hours of the world?

Mark

#14 RED PANTS

Believe it or not, this innocent fashion blunder can be credited for the birth of the *'Stuff Dutch People Like'* blog. We just couldn't wrap our heads around the sight of all the red-pant-wearing-folk. They were everywhere: riding bikes, sitting on terraces and parading down the streets (and no, we're not talking about the "hipster-red-pants" either).

Red pants are a unique Dutch offense. The first time you see a well-groomed older gent proudly sporting a bright yellow sweater and crimson red trousers (à la Ronald McDonald) you too will marvel at his boldness.

NOT TOO LONG AFTER MY RED-PANT EPIPHANY MY FATHER CAME TO VISIT ME IN AMSTERDAM. ONE AFTERNOON, AFTER HIS VARIOUS CITY-STROLLING EXPLOITS HE CASUALLY REMARKED, "SEEMS LIKE RED JEANS ARE IN FASHION HERE. MAYBE I SHOULD GET A PAIR?". SAY IT WASN'T SO! THE PREDILECTION APPEARED TO BE CONTAGIOUS! MY FATHER CERTAINLY WAS IN THE RIGHT TARGET DEMOGRAPHIC (55 +, WHITE, AND MALE) BUT HE SEEMED TO HAVE CAUGHT THE VIRUS AFTER ONLY A FEW MEAGER DAYS OF EXPOSURE. HOW IRRESPONSIBLE OF ME TO LET HIM GO OUT UNSUPERVISED!

It is important to note that this phenomena is not strictly limited to the sanguine variety. Dutchies have also been known to like citrus flavoured pants. You will catch long-legged Dutch men clad in orange, yellow, peach, or even pink trousers!

Don't take these judgments to heart though. If you're Dutch and you love your red pants, wear them proudly! After all, how else will foreigners be able to tell you apart from the Germans?

WHAT OUR COMMUNITY HAS TO SAY

The "red trousers man" is so much a typically Dutch phenomenon that it has become already a topic of cabarets, columnists and bloggers! There was even an item about it the other day on a TV special about Dutch humour. But it's typical of middle-aged, wealthy men, of the boring, non-hip type. If you lived outside 't Gooi, Bloemendaal, Oud-Zuid…

Caro

Karen

My parents got married in matching red corduroy pants back in 1982. My mother had a good collection of brightly coloured pants. We called them happy pants since the general colours of pants are very drab.

Martijin

The red trousers are usually only worn by so-called 'kakkers'. In fact, wearing the red pants almost automatically makes you a kakker.

I've studied this pretty carefully, and can supply some insights. The red trousers should be accompanied by either a pink or otherwise pastel button-collar or polo shirt, and the look is correctly completed leather boating shoes worn without socks, or possibly driving shoes. Often paired with a bright yellow sweater worn tied around the shoulders, or else a casual blazer with patch pockets.

It's essentially the Dutch version of the American Preppy phenomenon, WASP-y elite universities and prep-schools. It then trickled down to the masses—those aspiring to look like they came from that background, or who had attained the minimum of financial success required to pass. The mixture of influences and resources include golf, tennis and yacht-wear, and the demand is fed by the holy trinity of Ralph Loren, Brooks Brothers, Lacoste. Copy-cat brands such as Tommy Hilfiger and home-grown Dutch brand McGregor are considered low-rent versions, fit only for aspiring middle-managers.

I'm really surprised that this is considered a Dutch look, as the same phenomenon exists in an only slightly less-brash expression in both the French and the Italian bourgeois. The strangest part is really that the English public-school middle class—upon whom the American preppies modeled themselves—don't take it nearly as far, tending instead towards drab tones of the tweed and Wellies "country" set.

Capitein

Clairevl

I love red pants! My daddy often wears them (and he wears other bright pants as well, like orange, green, bright blue..) and always convince my little brother to wear them too. I think a red pants is sexy on a man!

Wendy

I'm sorry to say this, but this observation of yours is just a load of crap. All of the others so far I agree with, but it looks like you just made this one up.

Lisette

It is the uniform of the Dutch nouveau riche who want to show how important they are or how much money they have.

Desirée

Wendy, just because you've never seen these men, doesn't mean they aren't there. It might be a good idea for you to first read at least some of the comments, so you can see that they seem to be bound to particular regions of the country.

EJ

These originated as red sailing pants – it used to be that only those who had sailed across the Atlantic wore them. Over here, they seem to be for the posh set or those who like to think or pretend they are part of this set.

#15 NATURAL BIRTH

EIGHT YEARS AGO IN A SMOKY BROWN CAFE, I LOOKED ACROSS A PLATE OF BITTERBALLEN AND TOLD MY THEN-BOYFRIEND, "YES, I COULD LIVE HERE... BUT I WOULD NEVER EVER GIVE BIRTH IN THIS COUNTRY!" I JUST COULDN'T GET MY HEAD AROUND THE DUTCH "YOU MUST BIRTH AT HOME IN YOUR BATHTUB WHILE BURNING SAGE" ATTITUDE. MY FIRST DUTCH DOCTOR WAS OBSESSED WITH THE NOTION OF "BIRTH GEZELLIGHEID". DURING MY APPOINTMENTS, SHE WOULD CONTINUALLY TELL ME ABOUT HER UPCOMING LABOUR AND HOW SHE PLANNED TO GIVE BIRTH AT HOME BY CANDLELIGHT, ACCOMPANIED BY HER FAVOURITE MUSIC.

MY EARLY-TWENTIES-SLIGHTLY-JUDGMENTAL-NORTH-AMERICAN-SELF COULD ONLY MUSTER THE THOUGHT, "OMG, IS SHE PART OF SOME DUTCH HIPPY COMMUNE?? TIME FOR A NEW DOCTOR!"

AFTER MOVING NEIGHBOURHOODS (AND DOCTORS) I REALIZED THAT SHE WAS NOT PART OF A COMMUNE BUT SIMPLY SHARED THE AVERAGE DUTCH OPINION, THAT BIRTH WAS "NOT A MEDICAL CONDITION", AND AS SUCH, DID NOT REQUIRE EXTRANEOUS MEDICAL INTERVENTIONS.

FLASH FORWARD 8 YEARS AND I HAVE GIVEN BIRTH NATURALLY IN AMSTERDAM À LA DUTCH, ACCOMPANIED BY A FABULOUS DOULA, SUPER COMPETENT MIDWIVES, AND A SUPPORTIVE HUBBY! LESSON LEARNED: NEVER SAY NEVER!

There is no denying that Dutch people like to do things the "natural" way, the "real way" and the "normal" way. In fact, the majority of Dutchies are downright obsessed with making sure their behavior (and the behaviour of others) follows some unwritten rules of normalcy and realness. It should come as no surprise then, that this preoccupation with "keeping it real" extends to all acts – birth being no exception!

Dutchies are pioneers of the modern-day home birth. Although numbers have decreased over time (and sadly continue to) a hefty 25% of all births in the Netherlands occur at home (with another sizable percentage attempting to do so). Compare this to the less than 2% in France, Belgium, Germany and the UK and you can see why this is indeed a very Dutch thing.

Of course, doing so in the comfort of home also implies doing so without body-numbing and mind-altering substances. Is that a gasp we hear? Yes sir, Dutch women are a tough breed and notorious for their drug-free births. Even in the hospital, only 6% of Dutch women have an epidural. Across the Atlantic things are precisely the opposite. A recent study states that only 6% of women in large American hospitals opt for drug-free births.

C-SECTION RATE

15%
NETHERLANDS
(LOWEST IN OECD)

VS **32%**
USA

Are Dutch women genetically superior? Do they just not feel the pain like the rest of the world? Has all that cheese gone to their heads? Or are they seriously just tougher? The truth is rather simple: Dutch women have significantly less fear of childbirth pain and they accept it to be a natural part of the experience.

A Dutch pamphlet handed out to women during their pregnancies proudly informs, *"Giving birth hurts. Pain is a normal part of labour so expect it"*. Dutch society has managed to maintain the ever-important knowledge that childbirth is, in fact, the most natural part of our existence and something not to be feared or unnecessarily interfered with.

WHAT OUR COMMUNITY HAS TO SAY

I'm such a baby, I don't even like going to the dentist without drugs let alone give birth. Enjoy this wonderful new chapter in your life. Lisa

Lisa

I would choose giving birth over a visit to the dentist any day Yes, natural, being dutchie and all.

Jolan

lol i am a dutch outside holland and will have my baby abroad. When i told my doctor i wanted a natural birth she asked me if i really wanted to have all this pain, and why!!

Simone

Kudos to you for trying, and going drug free! And congrats. I, as a Dutchie, am baffled by all the options women in the US have. Epidural, laughing gas... I suppose to us it seems US women are either very afraid of pain, or are slightly 'alleen de lusten, niet de lasten' How to translate this... 'just the fun, not the pain' doesn't quite cut it, but I think you get my drift. To us, it has always been normal to have home deliveries. And no, these aren't all with candles and bath tubs, usually they are just in the comfort of your own bed, in your own home, which makes you feel more relaxed than being in some sterile, impersonal room in a hospital. And home deliveries are just as safe as hospital ones, and when a doctor has an inkling you might get complications, you will be referred to the hospital ahead of the delivery anyway.

Desirée

I'm an American in the Netherlands too, with a Dutch hubby of my own. I recently gave birth 5 months ago, and I too went 'au naturel'. When I told my (Dutch) co-workers, they would said, "Ah, yes, that's good." But when I told my family in America, they were like, "OMG?! More power to you!"

Emma

This is so true! I'm a Dutchie living in the US, and I will never forget the look my doctor gave me in the hospital – my little girl was breeched and my water broke: I asked him if I could try and give birth naturally. He must have thought I had gone insane, and couldn't get me in the operating room fast enough. Still very disappointed....and it's been more than seventeen years.

Florence

I never thought of my homebirth as a nod to my Dutch relatives, but now I will My mother moved to America before I was born and gave birth in hospital, but labored in the parking lot until after midnight so she wouldn't have to pay for an extra day (even though she got a discount for working in the accounting department of the hospital)–so Dutch-ly stubborn and frugal.

Familyride

My wife delivered at home in our own bed. All natural, no drugs, no sterile surroundings. Now I'm not going to voice an opinion on what is best (home/hospital) since I'm not the one who had to go through the pain, but what she said afterwards was something like: The beauty of birth outweighs the pain. Delivering at home adds greatly to this beauty so getting drugged is for, and I quote, "zeikwijven". All I can say is I never respected my wife as much as during that period.

Tom

Wonderful article! I had one baby with an epidural and HATED it! Had my second drug-free in a hospital and it was the best experience of my life! There is a reason why there are so many c-sections and inductions in the U.S. and it is because we over-medicate what doesn't need to be medicated at all. Drug-free means less interference means less complications. The rest of the world could learn a lot from the way the Dutch do birth!

Rylaarsdam

It is a very primitive way of giving birth! Numbers of home births and drugfree births are going down for a reason…. the realization that there is a better way! I am Dutch and have had 4 kids, one without drugs and the other 3 with drugs and these births were stress-free and as relaxed as can be, hence happier memories!

Alexandra

My husband is a Dutch citizen and he has never, nor will he ever, take Novocain when having a dental procedure. And don't even offer an aspirin for a headache!

Charlene

The birthing professionals and such all push for the natural births, as well as all the older Dutch women. But I find that the younger Dutch women nowadays are more likely to go for the rugprik (epidural) if they are not really afraid of needles. In a sense I find that the younger generation are getting more Americanized too.

Emma

This makes me feel so honored about being Dutch! I do find it odd that most Dutch women fail to breastfeed when they go the natural way in giving birth.

PDtje

#16 ZWARTE PIET

You know it's that time of the year again in Holland when you are greeted by a Dutch person on the street whose face is painted completely black and is sporting an afro wig, bright red lips and a colourful clown-like costume.

Stranger so is the fact that most Dutch people find this to be a completely normal and acceptable occurrence. Yes, Dutch people love their *Zwarte Piets* (Black Peters)!

Throughout November and early December the beloved *Zwarte Piet* icon is ubiquitous in the Netherlands and can be found manically smiling away at every turn (think grocery store flyers, posters, window displays, television commercials, wrapping paper, candy and so on). The painted black face image is inescapable.

Many western foreigners living or visiting Holland are horrified by such images. Why? Because they immediately conjure up images of American Blackface, a theatrical practice of the 19th century which propagated racist stereotypes and the mockery of African slaves and which appropriately ceased to exist once the Civil Rights Movement of the 1960s came into play. Thus, the existence of a modern day Blackface icon can be associated and/or confused with the racist stereotypes and degrading propaganda of yesteryear.

Sinterklaas, the origin of the modern Santa Claus, is said to have derived from St. Nicolaus, the Bishop of Mira, Turkey. According to the legend St. Nicolaus saved the town from starvation, revived 3 dead children, and offered gifts of dowries to poor girls in the village. However, the roots of the *Zwarte Piet* are simply unclear. Some say these merry helpers of Sinterklaas are simply black in colour after having gone down the chimneys to deliver presents (oh really?). Others explain they are "hired helpers", or dark because they come from Spain... (what few Dutchies will admit to is that *Zwarte Piet* may be based on enslaved Moors from North Africa...)

Regardless of the explanation, *Zwarte Piet's* very presence annually ignites a heated debate amongst Dutch people, tourists, expats and the immigration communities of the Netherlands. Is *Zwarte Piet* a harmless childhood tradition not worth debating or is it an archaic offensive character that no longer has a place in a multicultural society? We'll leave that up to you to decide!

WHAT OUR COMMUNITY HAS TO SAY

What often surprises me is the Dutch people's inability to anticipate how things are taken by others. "We didn't mean any offence, so it's your problem that you feel offended", is not a very good attitude as global citizens. Piets' problems are the act of caricaturing – not just the dark skin, but the afro hair, thick red lips, etc., are racial characteristics having been exaggerated – it's a derogative to make vicious fun of certain groups of people. If somebody picks my racial characteristics and caricatured them, I would feel offended. "We didn't mean any offence" doesn't work, because I know there was a clear intention to offend me. In a similar manner, the Zwarte Pieten tradition needs to examine what it's referring to. It's difficult to discuss especially when children are having fun, and we all love them, but this tradition is teaching them that they can be excused of anything if they declare "no offence intended". Dat kan niet?!

Reggie

Zwarte Piet is black, true, but he is also one of the most beloved traditional figures! Maybe I'm too narrow-minded and love Zwarte Piet too much, but I honestly can't understand how anyone can be offended by Zwarte Piet. He's just cool!

Cootje

This brings back memories from my childhood. I was always the one who was Zwarte pietdue to the fact I was black (from East Africa). But it didnt bother me at all. I always loved Sinterklaas. Lots of presents and pepernoten. YUM.

anoniem

63

The large immigrant population should not be offended by the tradition. They should accept it. Nobody is forced to celebrate Sinterklaas. Holland is a free country and also the traditions of other countries are accepted. That is the thing that SHOULDN'T change about Holland in this world that is getting less and less free.

Dutchie Abroad

I agree with Dutchie abroad, it's a tradition that we have, if immigrants feel offended by this, sorry to just say this but too bad. How about a dutch blond girl wanting to be in a bikini on the beach in an Arabic country, she would be imprisoned because of there traditions/culture, so she just simply wouldn't do that out of respect (and maybe a bit of fear)..We have our traditions in the Netherlands, respect those as we respect the traditions in other countries!

Just another Dutch living abroad

When I was a kid I didn't see Zwarte Piet as a black person. (Even though I'm coloured myself). He's just black because of the chimney dust. Well, that's what my parents told me. So, I believed that because it's all part of the mystery. And I love the idea that Zwarte Piet could squeeze himself through the narrow pipe.So, I agree. There's no need to start this discussion about racism every year. Zwarte Piet is just Zwarte Piet. And we all love him.

Sabaï

You don't have to celebrate it, but at least respect the fact that it's a part of the country's culture. If another country had a festivity that included black people dressed like white people, it would not offend me in the slightest.

Kim

Heh, I once did see an actual black person being dressed up as Zwarte Piet. And I must say that he had the most fun of them all because he didn't have to worry about his make-up messing up =PAnd well… there was that one time during 'Sinterklaas' that I heard a little kid (3 years old or so) was calling a random black person Zwarte Piet. The mother was embarrassed to the core, but the black guy just thought it was funny.

Ki

No one really knows where they came from, maybe st. nicholas just had black servants. Anyway, it's not intended racially, zwarte pieten aren't seen as black people as in the race. Everyone I know really did hear as a child that they got black from the soot in the chimneys. And Americans can go about it being racist all they want, you do not mess with Sinterklaas.

Eefje

Actually, you don't need to be white, to paint your face black, coloured or black people paint themselves black as well. Btw, ever noticed that he doesn't have a gender either. Women/girls who play Zwarte Piet do not become Zwarte Petra or something like that. Zwarte Piet is just Zwarte Piet.

Corine

When i was young, i always wanted to be a zwarte piet when i grew up! And i know there are a lot of 'white' kids who have the same ambition. I cant's imagine anything racist in zwarte pieten! I'm a teacher now (not a zwarte piet, too bad!). In my class i have 10 kids, where 1 has dutch parents. The rest of the kids is mostly Moroccan or Turkish. But they all!! love sinterklaas and zwarte piet.

Marijke

I'd say that modern Sinterklaas-events are race-related, but not racist. The modern day Zwarte Piet is just a fun children's character, who would not be seen as problematic if he was an elf or a talking animal. [...]The modern day Sinterklaasviering is a continuation of a once racist tradition in a form that is adapted to be as least racist as possible, while retaining our national cultural heritage. It is very difficult to keep one's own cultural heritage, while trying to not be offensive to people with other backgrounds. So I'd say Sinterklaas isn't inherently racist, but it isn't a totally innocent tradition either.

Furby

Apparently, and this forum shows it, it is hard for us Dutchies to take criticism on a national tradition so well-loved. That is a shame, because self-reflection is important, especially when people feel hurt. Two factors keep the tradition as it is: 1) We see no harm in it. Black petes are loved! They are seen as heroes by children (many of whom want to be Black pete's when they are young). 2) We were all raised with it. When you have such fond childhood memories about this tradition, you do not want to change it. Sinterklaas is a children's party, it is about family and love, all very positive notions, our substitute for the way people celebrate Christmas in the USA. It is hard to change such a tradition. It might feel like betraying your childhood, your parents (because if you change it: did they do anything wrong?) and deprive your children of what you had as a child. This is not to say this is correct or right, is it just how it feels.

Arjen

Haha I love this discussion! It used to be racism, but we don't see it as racism, we don't tell our children it's racism and JUST want to keep the fun part of the tradition alive. I even thought of a solution: It would be strange if a Zwarte Piet would be white all for sudden, but when children see a spot of Piet that is not painted black the parents say: "He comes through the chimney, why would he get black behind his ear?" and this is something children immediately believe most of the times. If the Pieten would get a BIT less black every year and have more spots the modern idea we all support of the black because of the chimney would make the racist part disappear. Many people think my theory is bullshit and that Zwarte Piet should stay Zwart. What do you think of this 'solution'?

Jessy

Always a polarizing issue! I am annually amazed by the effect my personal views about Zwarte Piet have on my Dutch friends. Normally open minded and cross-culturally aware folk who have travelled and lived across the globe have an incredibly strong reaction to my discomfort with the image. I don't stop my kids dressing as ZP, I have ZP toys in the house and I wouldn't dream of telling my adopted neighbours to paint their Piet a different colour. But as soon as I voice my disquiet about the whole thing I get an earful of "Dutch directness"! Clearly a sensitive nerve tweaked…

Erica

Well at least we are talking… However, first of all I have to admit one thing: I am Dutch and I love zwarte piet. Why do I love zwarte piet? Because I was born here and we have celebrated it since I was little. As far as I can remember, I never associated it with any kind of racism, and I consider myself to be very open minded. These are all opinions and feelings. Therefore subjective and only representative for me, a twentysomething year old white male dutchie.

However, I am equally convinced that it is impossible to historically separate zwarte piet and racism. In my opinion both camps are right. Zwarte piet is technically racist, but it has not had this meaning for a very long time. Therefore the meaning of what zwarte piet stands for has changed over time.

For me sinterklaas without zwarte piet would be like thanksgiving without a turkey.

J

This is always such a difficult topic! Being Dutch I love all 'zwarte piets'! (I was and am afraid of that scary old man though). On the other hand, I can imagine that non-Dutchies are horrified by this whole tradition. For them it's clearly related to our prominent role in slavery. And do I need to remind you that 'apartheid' is a Dutch word?I think all Dutch people (including me) are delusional when it comes to Sinterklaas and Zwarte Pieten. We have all been brought up with this tradition, don't see harm in it and we all love it. It's so deeply rooted in our culture, that it's difficult to see it from another perspective.

I have an idea, maybe you (yes you, dear blogger), can start a competition on this blog to choose a new worthy replacement for Zwarte Piet! Just a thought....

Simea

How about Santa Clause and his elves? Isn't that racism? A fat white guy using a race of elves to his needs? This is seen as 'ok' yet Sinterklaas and Petes isn't? To me it boils all down to the same. So yes, black Petes is racism. So is the use of elves. They are a race too by the sheer definition of a race.

Johan

The Dutch are not concerned about what others think of Black Pete as it is one of the best traditions in Holland and we will not be moved by ignorant comments. It is joyful period of presents and candy for children.

Ivo

Hi I've been reading all this crap about Zwarte Piet, wel of niet. (hee dat rijmt:)) Why don't you all just get a life !!!

Gerritje

You don't think life is about communication with people who disagree with you? Talking about things which offend or hurt others and what your reaction should be? Are there more important things than that? I'd like to know what you think they are....

Fee

#17 STROOPWAFELS

You can't visit/live in The Netherlands for long without stumbling across the famous *stroopwafel*. It sounds fairly medieval, but in reality it is a modern day tasty treat. *Stroopwafels* are made from two very thin layers of baked batter with a caramel-like filling in the middle. Stroll through any busy Dutch market, and you will smell the delicious confections long before you actually see them being made.

Ever notice how a Dutch person places their *stroopwafel* so that it sits perfectly balanced on their coffee mug? This is the traditional way to eat one, so that the rising steam from the hot beverage warms the waffle and slightly softens the inside, making it all yummy and melty on one side and crispy on the other.

Stroopwafels are said to have originated in the late 18th century in the town of Gouda, made famous for its cheese. Be careful though, as they are highly addictive. Take that first bite, at your own risk. Beware too of the pre-packaged types of *stroopwafels* found at grocery or tourist stores. They may have sat on the shelves for months. If you enjoy the taste of sweetened cardboard, and are not worried about losing any teeth, then plunge right in! Otherwise, head to your nearest local market to find the real deal.

WHAT OUR COMMUNITY HAS TO SAY

Even better: stroopwafelkruimels (stroopwaflecrumbs)

Krullevaar

Stroopwafelkruimels with plain yoghurt is lovely. I introduced my family to stroopwafels (sitting them over a hot beverage of course) and now I have to send them regularly to Turkey to my mum (lucky thing retired there) and to England to the rest of my family. Hmmmm, maybe I should stop and then they will come visit me. A by-product of coming for the stroopwafels of course.

Jenarla

Our local McDonalds even does a stroopwafel McFlurry!

Sam

Man, I tried the weirdest stroopwafel this weekend, besides the stroop it also had bacon and rosemary. Insanely tasty! And there I was thinking the Dutch were incapable of making nice food!

Stefmanovic

An alternative and waaaay more effective method of heating them up is to chuck them in a hot oven for a minute or so. Or say, 10/15 seconds in a microwave. Yumyum! Don't burn you tongue on the caramel though! They're not actually made from two waffles though. A small ball of batter (Or dough. It's more the thickness of dough in my opinion) is placed in a waffle iron and then baked. The resulting waffle is then sliced open to add the caramel inbetween the two halves.

Van Loo

tip: when you bought the cardboard ones, put the in the microwave for just a few seconds at max Watt.

E

One of my guilty pleasures.

Elja

#18 BRING YOUR OWN CAKE

If you've spent any time in a Dutch office you will quickly notice an abundance of confectionery goods. The larger the office, the more often cake will mysteriously appear around the coffee machine. The workings of a generous boss with a sweet tooth? Nope, it's the endearing Dutch tradition of eating cake on your birthday, no matter what your age. Sounds normal enough, right? But the Dutch twist on this tradition is that you are expected to buy and bring your own cake to the party! Here you were thinking that birthdays were all about you! Guess again!

In the land of the Dutchies, it is never appropriate to assume someone will bring a cake for you on your special day. More importantly, do not think you can quietly avoid this tradition at work. If it's your birthday the office manager, HR department and even the Director is certain to know about it and you will certainly not make new friends or impress the colleagues by attempting to usurp this ever important socio-cultural norm. Bring in your own cake, take in all the *gefeliciteerds*, do a lot of 3-kisses and enjoy yourself!

The standard Dutch birthday cake is normally a pastry tart topped with assorted fruit and whipped cream, commonly referred to as vlaai. On birthdays a variety of delicious cakes are available and appropriate, including *appeltaart* (apple pie), *Limburgse vlaai*, (pie with fruit filling), *peperkoek* (gingerbread) and even *spekkoek* (layered cake from Indonesia).

Not a great baker? Not to worry – there are a multitude of Dutch businesses that are supported solely by the fact that every working citizen has to buy at least one birthday cake a year. Do the maths folks that's over 10 million *vlaai* a year!

WHAT OUR COMMUNITY HAS TO SAY

The principle of "trakteren" is being practised by the very young. Even in pre school (kindergarten?) parents arrange candy / cake / whatever, for the kids to share with their classmates in school. The teacher will make a birthday hat for the lucky kid, and make the kid walk to other teachers in the school to give them a piece of the pie / cake as well. This happens with 5 – 12 year olds. (or at least it did in my days), as you can see… trakteren is part of our culture. It's considered polite and social, but we do make sure we mention it before dropping by someone's house of course.

Robert

Oh my Gosh! This is Hilarious!!!So true!!! I have to say that working in the office, this was my least favorite part. Not only because you feel obligated on bringing something, but your colleagues keep on asking about it and they can give you a very uncomfortable feeling if you are taking too long on getting something! On my first birthday i had a colleague coming to my desk and asking me if i would like her to go with me to get something? I was like: WHAT??? The whole kissing… WOW… really is that really necessary? The funny part is that everybody in my office hates the whole Congratulations part and the whole singing "Lang zal die leven, Lang zal die leven" but nobody says anything to stop it! The same people complain everytime someone has a birthday but they just go on and on…. I really don't get it!

Rosana

I'm Dutch but I now live in Texas, and I was shocked to see that in America, once you're an adult your birthday hardly gets celebrated. Not only no 'trakteren' (maybe you can write a post about the closer relationship people in the workplace have in Holland), but no birthday parties. Only when you're thirty or forty or fifty, preferably work funereal over-the-hill decorations. My husband said it would be weird to invite people to my birthday because then they'd feel they had to buy a present. It's just not done. I miss Dutch birthdays, not just mine, but my friends' birthdays. It was much more gezellig!

Barbara

Yereth
I'm a Dutch living in China, and funnily enough here having your birthday basically means you're going to be treating all your friends to whatever activity undertaken (dinner, karaoke, a night out drinking or all of the above). We're not alone in the tradition!

Shelley
I really dislike this custom. I'm from Mississippi and back home you get spoiled on your birthday however old you are. Here in Rotterdam i've found myself sweating it out in the damn kitchen for a day or two and filling everybody's glasses and cleaning up afterwards. I really adore entertaining, but on my birthday, i want to be the Queen! I do however enjoy the kissing part. : D

Vliegende Hollander
I was managing a team of 6 in the office I was in, and even though I was bedridden with sickness on my birthday and answering emails only from home, they INSISTED that I come into the office and bring cake, as THEY didn't want to miss out on cake for my birthday. I had to travel for an hour with cake, sit and eat it (promptly threw it up again), then travel an hour back home…

coderofsalvation
I'm dutch and this is totally normal..it would be a total nightmare if you have to trust your friends on bringing a cake..it would be eaten before arrival!

#19 MASHING THEIR FOOD

For anyone reading this, it shouldn't come as a big surprise that Dutch food has yet to sweep the globe. Although pockets of Dutch dishes can be found scattered throughout the world, delectable Dutch cuisine has not really caught on.

"Fancy me picking up some Dutch food on the way home from work?" or *"Wow, you have got to try this new Dutch restaurant in SoHo!"* are phrases you may never hear uttered.

Isn't it odd that a nation of travelling, colonising, emigrating folk never managed to sow their own culinary seeds? C'mon, who are we kidding?? Even those emigrated Dutch settlers were thrilled to have found tastier grub!

Sure, New York was more than happy to take the Dutch names of Brooklyn (Breukelen), Harlem (Haarlem), Coney Island (from Konijneneiland) and Staten Island — but when it came to Dutch cuisine, they left it at the door (apart from the cheese that is)!

Dutch people have 3 very specific ways of preparing food/vegetables. They like to either:
a) mash the hell out of something,
b) boil the shit out of something, or
c) deep-fry the life out of something!

Let's discuss a). Dutch people's affinity for mashing. Dutch people love to mash; mash, mash and mash again! Case in point, the beloved stamppot. For those of you who are unaware of the stamppot, it actually combines two of the Dutch cooking specialties a) mashing and b) boiling. First you boil the shit out of various veggies (potatoes, carrots, etc.). Then you mash the hell out of them, throw a little sausage on the side, and voila, a perfect Dutch meal!

There are, of course, many more Dutch dishes - the *Zuurkoolstamppot* (sauerkraut mashed with potatoes), the *Andijviestamppot* (endive mashed with potatoes) or the Boerenkoolstamppot (kale mixed with mashed potatoes). Are you starting to see a pattern here?

The staying power of the stamppot is truly mind-boggling. The dish is said to be one of the oldest dishes, originating in the early 1600s, and yet somehow it still remains one of the most popular.

The good news is that traditional Dutch cooking requires no finesse, delicacy or precision. Throw caution to the wind, over boil those veggies, bring out your mashing skills, and tell your friends you are going Dutch!

STAMPPOT RECIPE
(SERVING 4)

1. PEEL POTATOES FOR 4 PERSONS. MAYBE SOME MORE. SO YOU WILL KEEP A LITTLE FOR A PRAKJE (LEFTOVERS) NEXT DAY

2. COOK IN SALTED WATER. WHILE THIS IS GOING ON. DICE UP A SLAB OF BACON. AND LET IT FRY TILL DESIRED CRISPNESS IN A TINY PAT OF BUTTER. IF YOU GOT A GOOD NO-STICK PAN YOU CAN EVEN FORGET ABOUT THE BUTTER.

3. WASH ABOUT 1 LBS. OF ENDIVES, MORE OR LESS DEPENDING ON HOW MUCH YOU LIKE THE GREENS. AND TEAR OR CUT UP THE LEAVES. IF YOU'RE A SPOILED BRAT LIKE ME YOU WILL LIKE TO CUT OUT THE CENTER NERVE OF THE GREEN LEAVES.

4. WHEN THE POTATOES ARE DONE COOKING. POUR OFF THE WATER. ADD A BIT OF NUTMEG (OR ANY SPICE IF YOU FEEL ADVENTUROUS) AND MASH THE POTATOES WITH ONE OR TWO DASHES OF MILK TO DESIRED MASHED-NESS. I LIKE TO ADD CHEESE, EITHER DICED OR SHREDDED. YOUNG GOUDA OR EDAMMER MAKES THE BEST FOR MELTING IN THE STAMP.

5. AT THE VERY LAST MOMENT BEFORE SERVING YOU CAN ADD THE ENDIVES AND THE BACON AND STIR IT ALL THROUGH. OF COURSE YOU COULD SERVE THIS WITH A ROOK WORST. BUT MYSELF. I PREFER A GEHAKTBAL (DUTCH MEATBALLS) WITH MY STAMP.

RECIPE BY LYNN

WHAT OUR COMMUNITY HAS TO SAY

You forgot the most important serving tip of the stamppot: het "kuiltje jus", the dip finish of gravy, the little hole in the stamppot made by the gravy-spoon to be filled with gravy !

PaulO

I use all kind of eastern spices (like coriander, ginger, hot pepper etc) and soysaus. I "mash" it together with the raw endive, the mashed potatoes and some cheese. Then I put some cheese on top and put it around 25 minutes in the oven until the cheese is melted. It's great!

Esther

My father thought me and now Ive taught my daugher: make a mountain of your stampot. From the top make little roads with your fork; all the way down.Then make a tiny pool in the top of the mountain for your gravy. All kids like to do this and makes eating stamppot even more fun!

Marlies

My parents make endive stamppot with raw endive, aardappel purree(from powder) and cheesesauce(also from powder), with meat, usually spekjes, mixed trough instead of rookworst served with it. I like it like that, like boerenkoolstamppot too, but not really a fan of hutspot altough I can eat it just for nutrition, but I rather eat my pants than zoorkoolstamppot, had it once and never again.

iemand

The carrots and onions mixed with potatoes is called 'hutspot'. In Leiden, where I'm from, this is eaten on the 3rd of October, when the 'leidenaren' were liberated from the Spanish occopation. It is a lovely dish, especially eaten on a cold day!

Ivonne

Don't forget: You have to eat everything out of the same plate. Soup as starter, scrape the heck out the plate. Put you stamppot in it, scrape scrape scrape and then pour your vla in the same plate. And all that is eaten with a spoon. That grosses me out. But love stamppot.

Es

Before the potato was known in Europe (and The Netherlands), they used parsnips instead for hutspot.

PJ

77

My parents grew up in Overijsel, Nederland and I was born near a small village in a boerderij. We had no electricity and no running water. During the summer the turf fed cooking stove went out to the schuur to be thoroughly cleaned and for several weeks (or months) my mother cooked on a one burner petroleum stel.

I believe this is the reason the stamppot was invented; to use one pot for everything was the only way to cook. I've lived in Canada now for 50+ years and still make stamppot occasionally as do all 3 of my children – it's comfort food. My favourite is with carrots and fried onions. My aunt made "stim stam" with raw endive and if anyone has a recipe for this I'd love to have it. My mother never deep fried anything, we only saw deepfrying when we moved to the West coast and it was at the markt where one could get patat.e endive stamppot with raw endive, aardappel purree(from powder) and cheesesauce(also from powder), with meat, usually spekjes, mixed trough instead of rookworst served with it.

I like it like that, like boerenkoolstamppot too, but not really a fan of hutspot altough I can eat it just for nutrition, but I rather eat my pants than zoorkoolstamppot, had it once and never again.

Johanna

#20 SKATING (ON NATURAL ICE)

On the odd occasion when frigid temperatures and snow hit the Netherlands, you are sure to hear Dutch people grumbling about how cold it is, how the snow is slowing down trains, how flights are not taking off from Schiphol airport and how long it took them to get to work - but secretly they love it.

They love the cold temperatures, the frosty wind, the snow-capped canal houses and the gleaming sunshine. They love it for the excitement it brings to an otherwise grey and dreary endless Dutch winter.

Couple the snow, the sun and the cold with the ultimate anticipation of skating on natural ice, and you have almost 16 million people on the brink of a national orgasm. Dutch people love to skate, but more importantly they love the elusiveness of skating on natural ice in the great outdoors.

Of course, being able to skate outdoors for a few days every few years is one thing, but add freezing temperatures and the *Elfstedentocht* to the mix and you have an entire country in the grips of joyful anticipation.

Haven't heard of the *Elfstedentocht?* The Eleven Cities Tour is an ice-skating marathon held in Friesland with participants happily skating through 11 Dutch towns on a mere 200 kilometers of natural ice paths. So popular is the *Elfstedentocht* that people have to win a spot in a national lottery in order to compete. In the past 20 years, the *Elfstedentocht* has happened only once, in 1997! The thought of it possibly happening again is therefore pretty darn freakin' exciting to these ice-loving/ice-skating people.

Weather-wise the odds are against them, but that doesn't stop Dutch people from wishing and hoping, and more importantly – practicing! Go to any rink or body of slightly frozen water in the middle of a cold Dutch winter and you will see scores of Dutchies sharpening their blades and practicing their moves in the hope of one day being able to participate in this historic 11 city race!

WHAT OUR COMMUNITY HAS TO SAY

In the past 30 years, the Elfstedentocht has happened all of three times: 1997, 1985 and 1986.

M V

My badass grandmother competed in the 1940s, when she was a hardcore athlete. She said that the Prince of Wales also competed.

Emily

They say you have to be Dutch to understand it, I was also surprised to see how much passion they put into it and how news is overwhelmed with information about how thick is the ice and how all people come together and help to take the snow away. Amazing!

Monique

Yep, people all over the world come to compete. There're limited places and there's a for-members-only-lottery that will decide who can compete/do the race.

Joris

I am a Dutchie. I just want to say that it is not true that everyone loves it. I hate the cold and I really don't care if there is coming a elfstedentocht!

Anouk

I've lived in Leeuwarden, the starting point and finish of the Elfstedentocht. I was there the last time, in 1997. It was awesome, but I didn't quite fathom the fact that I was witnessing a historic event. I'd love to go back again to see it all again with the same good friend as in 1997

Thijzzz

Don't forget our own King Willem-Alexander who participated in 1986 under the name of W.A. van Buren.

I just got back from skating on a lake and then saw this post :p I did feel very dutch today, as I cycled there, skated, and even ate a piece of cheese.

Eefje

#21 HERRING

Dutch people have a tremendous love affair with one particularly small, slippery, slimy, oily and smelly sea-creature, the hallowed Herring! To say that the Dutch like herring is a vast understatement.

Herring is a small, silvery-coloured fish found in the North Atlantic and North Pacific oceans. Dutch people began fishing and trading herring over 1,000 years ago and much of Holland's wealth and prolific history of sea trade can in fact be attributed to this tiny species. Business kicked into full swing in the 14th century when a Dutchman by the name of Williem Buekelszoon invented a tasty and popular process for curing the fish in brine.

FOR THOSE BRAVE ENOUGH TO GIVE IT A GO. IT'S IMPORTANT TO KNOW THAT THE VERY ACT OF EATING HERRING IS AN ART FORM IN ITSELF. TO GO DUTCH. YOU MUST GRAB THE FISH BY ITS TINY LITTLE TAIL. COCK YOUR HEAD BACK TO A SLIGHTLY UNCOMFORTABLE ANGLE AND TAKE ONE LARGE FISHY BITE. THIS DELIGHTFUL LITTLE PERFORMANCE HAS EVEN THE MOST HUMBLE OF DUTCH PERSONS BRIMMING WITH PRIDE.

Dutch people also make a big hoopla about the kickoff of the herring season. Every year the seaside city of Scheveningen celebrates the opening of the season with Vlaggetjesdag (Flag Day) and the first barrel is given to the King to sell at auction for charity. It's not unusual for the first precious herring barrel to sell for over €50,000!

How much do Dutch people really love herring? Well, they happily consume over 12,000,000 kilos every year! That's at least 5 slippery delights per person annually. Of course this begs the question - have you met your quota yet?

WHAT OUR COMMUNITY HAS TO SAY

Miss Neriss

Herring (and its equally slippery partner in crime, Eel) is something that I just can't stomach. I really want to be Dutch enough to eat it, but I just can't get it near my mouth! My (Dutch) husband loves it and can't get enough, but even he is a bit freaked out about the ritual of eating it all in one go…

Really fresh herrings don't need onions. The onions (and pickles in the Amsterdam region) were used to mask the pungent smell and foul taste of old (or rotting) herring. I love to eat herrings without onions. 4, sometimes 5 at a time. They are a perfect cure for hang-overs. Start your day with a few herrings and you're fit as a fiddle in no time

Martijn

Sitting here in the desert of Saudi Arabia with – you guessed it – a freezer full of herring. Love it!

Edwin

Since 2008 I live in Hawaii, and while there's literally great tasting fish all around me, both cooked and raw, there's one fish I truly miss: rauwe haring!
Well, make that two fishes.. I shouldn't forget about Kibbeling

Jeroen

It really depends on where you are. In Scheveningen for instance people ALWAYS eat herring using their hands (the traditional way), while in Amsterdam most people eat herring on toast/sandwiches with a fork and a knife. It's also the case that the closer you get to the coast, the more people seem to like herring. There are a lot of Dutch people who don't like it at all and think it's nasty. I love it though!

Lotte

Most herring is exported to Germany. But then, most of everything is exported to Germany (Dutch potatoes make up 30% of all German fries, for instance). 90% of herring is ground into fishmeal in Scandinavia. The English waged war over the fishing rights for herring.
Herring is consumed in a number of ways, salted, dried, smoked, fried, laid in herbs, cream, or white wine, and even wrapped around a pickle and laid in vinegar, but never really raw.

Ablabius

I could eat 5 herring every single day.. I love herring! rollmops! smoked! boiled! pickled! raw! DELICIOUS!!! And I'm English.. not Dutch. A love of herring is the gold standard of civilisation!

Mandy

#22 HAIR GEL

Dutch people are among the highest consumers of hair gel in the world. If you don't believe it, go and stand in the middle of any busy Dutch street and start counting. As the numbers start quickly adding up you will have no choice but to agree.

Not all Dutch douse their hair in this stuff but there are enough of them to skew the per capita consumption for the whole nation. It's hard to miss the guys with the blond curls slicked back on their head in a crunchy mess.

We cannot offer an explanation for the cause of this phenomena. Is it because Dutch men are too cheap to get a haircut? Is it easier to re-apply gel in the morning than actually wash your hair? Do Dutch men genuinely think the "semi-long-curly-blond-hair-dipped-in-copious-amounts-of-gel" is a hot look?

This crispy "Dutch hair" often belongs to a certain type of Dutchie. In recent years it seems to have become particularly popular with makelaars (real-estate agents), frat boys, bankers, students, field-hockey players, rowers, and beloved football players. You'll be able to either spot them on their scooters (the makelaars in particular), or on their boats or cycling through the city with their short stubby field-hockey sticks.

This look has even made it into the Urban Dictionary! They refer to these long greasy locks as the Dutch Prince look. Don't be fooled by the glamorous name, there is nothing royal about it!

WHAT OUR
COMMUNITY HAS TO SAY

I gotta be honest, since i was so used to our Dutch boys doing their hair like that (in holland i actually play fieldhockey) i was amazed to see that guys in America don't put anything in their hair at all! I've been living in upstate New York for almost a year now and i'm liking their hairdo wayy better. At least now i can put my hands in somebody's hair without getting stuck

Meritdeperit

American women like myself do NOT like shellacked hair. It's worse when the inevitable baldness sets in because the gel makes the man look like he has even LESS hair, arranged like stiff wires covering his head! Okay, maybe it helps waterproof the hair and keep it out of the face if it's windy, but in bed, PLEASE, wash it out first.

Amy

I have even seen that gel in the toilet of a restaurant… just in case the duck salad made your hair look fuzzy or something; toilet with a small sink with only cold water by the way. The Netherlands is just The Netherlands

Mr. Basquetard

The following theory came from a former roommate of mine, American himself: it's the only haircut that doesn't get messed up when you ride your bike.
Simple as that. Go with the spikes, the fringe, or anything else: it's all over the place as soon as you step off that oma fiets. Hair gelled back: not a millimeter of it has moved by the time you get to your destination, regardless of how crap the weather decides to be – and we all know that tends to happen way more often than needed.
Bike + wind + rain = one way out: aerodynamics.

Alexandre

My two year old son goes to kindergarten here. The first three months, every single day he would come home with hair gel in his hair! To the point we had to ask them to stop putting the stuff in his hair! Everyday for months they did... Unbelievable when you think about it...

Peter

Oh man, this is so true. My girlfriend and I are expats living in Rotterdam – the guys here can't get enough of the gelatinous mess! I mean there is "doing your hair" and then there's pouring a whole tub of gel on it in an attempt to look "hockey". The former makes you look nice, and the latter makes your head look like a slick backed car crash.

TomActive Backpacker

Bf and I have a term for this: BDH. It's exactly what you describe, Bad Dutch Hair.

JD

Haha this is so true! But I always think about foreigners who would walk in public with a sheep on their head it's just how you see it :p

Len

In formal occasions, it's an almost an un-outspoken rule that you look neat. Dutch people don't see messy curls as neat. Therefore, on occasion, I sometimes put some gel in my hair. People see that as neatness, like you are taking good care of yourself. Don't know where that came from, but that's how things stand. xD

Dutchmanjoel

Yeh, but honey, hair with lots of gel in it DOESN'T look neat, it looks like a big greasy mess! ;))

Dot

#23 JOKES ABOUT GERMANS AND BELGIANS

AFTER MY FIRST DAY OF WORK IN THE NETHERLANDS, I WAS DROPPED OFF AT THE LOCAL ABN-AMRO IN AMSTELVEEN TO OPEN A BANK ACCOUNT. A FRIENDLY DUTCH BANKER WELCOMED ME INTO HIS OFFICE, AND I WAS QUICKLY HANDED A STACK OF PAPERS TO SIGN. AS I SIGNED AWAY, THE DUTCH BANKER BUSIED HIMSELF WITH SMALL TALK. HE RATTLED THROUGH SOME OPENING TOPICS AND THEN ASKED IF MY LAST NAME WAS ORIGINALLY FROM GERMANY. THIS IMMEDIATELY SET OFF AN IMPROMPTU LESSON IN DUTCH HUMOUR AS HE RECITED A NEVER-ENDING SERIES OF DUTCH JOKES IN SLIGHTLY WONKY ENGLISH. I SMILED AND NODDED, SIGNING THE MASS OF PAPERS IN FRONT OF ME, LOOKING UP OCCASIONALLY TO SEE HIM RED-FACED, SIPPING ON A CARTON OF MILK AND LAUGHING AWAY TO HIMSELF. MOST OF THE JOKES WERE LOST IN TRANSLATION, HOWEVER AFTER HEARING THE FIRST FEW, I QUICKLY REALIZED THERE WAS A COMMONALITY AMONGST THEM – POKING FUN AT GERMANS. NOT SURE MY GERMAN GRANDFATHER WOULD HAVE BEEN LAUGHING!

Dutch people love to make jokes at the expense of their two favourite neighbours: the Belgians and the Germans! It's that good old "big brother, little brother" complex found amongst many bordering nations, mixed with some lingering historic animosity and a healthy dose of sport-related rivalry.

The Belgian jokes are generally light-hearted, whereas the German ones can be a bit more cutting and often involve tricking Germans into some form of bodily harm. A typical example:

> A DUTCH MAN SEES A MAN ON HIS KNEES USING HIS HAND TO DRINK WATER FROM ONE OF AMSTERDAM'S CANALS. HE WALKS UP TO HIM AND SAYS IN DUTCH "HEY – YOU CAN'T DRINK THAT WATER. IT'S DIRTY AND WILL MAKE YOU SICK".
> THE TOURIST SHOUTS BACK IN GERMAN: "WAS SAGEN SIE?" (WHAT ARE YOU SAYING?)
> THE DUTCH MAN RESPONDS IN GERMAN: "SIE SOLLEN MIT ZWEI HANDE TRINKEN. DAS GEHT BESSER!" (YOU SHOULD USE BOTH HANDS. IT'S MUCH BETTER!")

Funny enough, a lot of the jokes that the Dutch make about the Belgians are the exact same jokes the Belgians make about the Dutch (just reverse the nationalities)! The common themes include lack of intelligence and cheapness. The hard-hitters involve both.

WHAT OUR COMMUNITY HAS TO SAY

Ask Belgians about their Dutch jokes. They have at least the amount we have about Belgians.

I find that jokes about Belgians are "softer", like about a dim-witted younger brother, while those re: Germans can be quite mean.

Anja

Although it is true that some people are still quite sensitive about Germany because of the past and there is a high level of sports rivalry between the two countries, I think most jokes in the Netherlands are made about Belgians.

Jeroen

Jolene

We make jokes about Belgians (lack of intellect) and Belgians make jokes about the Dutch (being cheap).

After three years among Dutchies I have to say that the jokes about Germans are getting old. Maybe I'm too German but hearing bad jokes references day in and day out can be very tiring. We Germans on the other hand don't care that much about the Dutch and rather joke about Austrians, French or Poles.

Paul

Max

I feel embarrassed reading this as a Dutch girl...On the other hand it's quite common for every country to make jokes about neighbouring countries. The English have lots of jokes about the French and the Irish, don't they? I know the Germans joke about the Dutch as well, the Swedish make fun of Norwegians and the Danish, and so on.

Germans don't have jokes about the Dutch. Beating them at soccer is enough to make us happy.

Ouch!

Hahaha, touché!

Oscar

Wee

Jolene

Actually the Belgians make jokes about the Dutch people being stupid and they think we Dutchies joke about them being cheap. We both do the same jokes

Nienke

Nienke

#24 DAIRY

Dutch people like milk products, a lot. Even if you know very little about Dutch people or have just arrived in the Netherlands, you will soon observe the Dutch's predilection for dairy.

In most other cultures milk is only a staple of children's diets. As children age, milk is eventually phased out as their beverage of choice.

In the Netherlands, however, milk remains popular well into adulthood. Step into any Dutch office lunchroom and you will be confronted by rows of Dutch men and women happily slurping on cartons of milk at meal time. Apparently the Dutch did not get the (North American) memo that milk is only for children.

Pair a simple cheese sandwich with a carton of *melk* and you are now consuming the nation's most popular luncheon meal!

Need proof of this penchant? Just look at their height! The Dutch tower over all nations and are now the tallest people in the world. The average adult male in the Netherlands is 6 feet 1 inch (1.85 m). Dutch people's height appears to be contagious: immigrants living in the Netherlands are taller on average than their home-bred counterparts.

After all, as the popular Dutch television adverts' proclaim: *Melk moet!* (Milk is a must!)

72% OF DUTCH CHEESE IS EXPORTED
(3RD LARGEST CHEESE EXPORTER)

LIST OF DUTCH CHEESE
• EDAM • GOUDA • LEERDAMMER • LEYDEN • MAASLANDER • MAASDAM • PARRANO

WHAT OUR COMMUNITY HAS TO SAY

The most popular type of milk is 'Halfvolle melk' followed by 'Volle melk'. 'Karnemelk' is in third place. Source: Worked in a supermarket for 3 years.

Muffer

Once when I was working for an international consulting firm, we had our colleagues from Brussels over in Amsterdam for a work lunch. Being the junior, I had to do all the work AND had to arrange the lunch. Being Dutch, I naturally arranged for a simple cheese sandwich and karnemelk. One of the senior partners impolitely declined eating anything and said 'that's so Dutch'.

mrds

What about VLA??? The finest and most Dutch dairy EVER. Available in all kinds of flavours, like chocolate, vanilla, strawberry, caramel. A very important Dutch thing!!!! Very.

mrds

Haha! Same thing here! I also asked for a 'bruine boterham met kaas' when I came back from an amazing India trip, including the best food I ever had. Nothing beats a whole wheat sandwich with cheese & milk

acolade

As a 110% Dutchman I have to agree to loving dairy as well, couple of liters of milk per week, 2 cartons of yoghurt and the occasional vla. So far fresh milk (pasturised) has been the only thing I've missed when living abroad/traveling. I even had my friends bring me a "bruine boterham met kaas & melk" (whole wheat sandwich with cheese & milk) when they picked me up at Schiphol after a 5 month trip through South East Asia. Even though Thailand has the best cuisine I've ever tried it became quite difficult to go without simple things as whole-wheat bread & fresh milk.

Marieke

I have been living in the UK for more than 15 years and I do have to admit that one of the things I miss most here is the Dutch dairy, including our delicious cheese. The dairy aisles in the supermarkets here just do not compare to what is available back home, with ever new appearing flavours of vla and so many varieties of yogurts. My children find it a veritable feast as well and eating vla at the end of the evening meal is one of the highlights of their day when on holiday. At the end of the holiday I always raid the local Albert Heijn to buy several kilos of vacuum packed cheese. I wish I could bring back a car boot full of karnemelk as well, but that's a bit more tricky...

Angela

#25 GOING CAMPING

Every year in July an exodus hits the Lowlands. Dutch people flee their flat little country *en-masse*. The oddity isn't so much that they are leaving (who can blame them?) but the fact that Dutch people exit in a very peculiar, yet strikingly similar manner. Come 17:30 sharp on a Friday they hit the highways in their fully stocked car or caravan brimming with supplies.

What on earth is happening? And where are these thousands of Dutch people headed? It's *VAKANTIE TIJD!*

Dutch people vacation in a practically identical fashion: Caravan? Check! Tents? Check! Dutch flag? Check! *Pindakaas, hagelslag, beschuit*, toilet paper? Check, check, check and check! It is not an uncommon sight to see a group of Dutch people in a campsite in Spain enjoying solely Dutch food. Don't believe us? According to the Dutch news site NCR, Dutchies are obsessed with bringing their favourite goods from home!

WHAT DO THE DUTCH BRING ON VACATION?

LIQUORICE	HAGELSLAG	PEANUT BUTTER	TOILET PAPER	CHEESE

48%	47%	37%	56%	49%
OF DUTCHIES BRING IT ALONG	OF DUTCHIES CAN'T LEAVE HOME WITHOUT IT	OF DUTCHIES STUFF IT IN THEIR SUITCASE	OF DUTCHIES SHOVE IT BETWEEN THE SEATS	FLING IT IN THEIR TRUNKS

Of course you may be wondering why the Dutch need to bring their own food (or toilet-paper) on vacation – well, you can't expect there to be good food in the top-culinary locales of the world can you? We are going to assume that it must be their fear of not getting a decent meal (or wipe) abroad, instead of their infamous reputation for "thriftiness"!

Apart from similar modes of transport and tastes, the Dutch also collectively vacation in the same holiday destinations. If you are Dutch and heading on a summer vacation you must pick either France, Germany or Spain. Feeling really wild? Why not give Italy or (gasp) Scandinavia a try!

We see you shaking your heads, thinking *"Well, some Dutch do this, but certainly NOT all of us!"* Well folks, it was estimated that nearly 4 million Dutch people pack up their tents and toilet-paper and take the highly exotic camping vacation just described above. You'll be sure to spot the Dutch in the campgrounds by the abundance of blond-haired blue-eyed children running wildly about. You also can't miss the familiar Dutch flag flying from the caravan roofs. God forbid they would ever be confused for a bunch of Germans!

WHAT OUR COMMUNITY HAS TO SAY

As much as I am willing to integrate into Dutch society, I draw the line at camping and caravan holidays! A nice hotel in an exotic location with great food or three weeks cooped up in a tent where I have to walk miles to have a shower and cook my own supper. Tough choice. My partner used to go camping in Italy every year when he was younger. I once asked him why on Earth they would travel all the way to Italy just to stay at a campsite with other Dutch folk. His reply: "There weren't just Dutch people. There was also many people from Germany and Belgium". Sigh...

Kelly M

There is one more camping destination: Belgium.I worked on a Dutch camping in Belgium for 2 years. I am saying "Dutch camping" because majority of guests were Dutch. Funny thing about them is that once they arrive on a destination and place their caravan and tents they stay there for entire 2 weeks! I thought the idea of camping was to move from place to place…

Paulina

Ah, yes… Walking to the lavatories, in a dressing gown, with a roll of toiletpaper underneath your arm… Brings back fond memories !

Sjess

I'm Dutch, and a bit ashamed of the trend of my fellow campers to camp in essential ENCLAVES along the French and Spanish Mediterranean coast. My guess for the reason we move out with caravans and tents is so we can spend the full three week vacation time many adults here get somewhere away. So there you have it, one family of five, three weeks in a tent or two or a caravan on or near a camping (campsite) …. affordable price.
I agree a lot of us like to go to particular places 'together' either to keep a sense of security or simply to hide from the inevitable awkward moment when we don't speak the local native language. There are some odd things going on in our heads I agree. But I will defend my pride as a Dutchman when someone implies a very practical and undeniably necessary precaution against whining kids is just a cheap way to save money.

Joost

Don't forget to bring the mayonnaise….. because how else will you eat the potatoes? and as my family used to say: "you can not get good mayonnaise abroad, it's just to sour".

nomynot

I agree that a lot (read: way to many) dutch people will take a caravan on holiday, but don't forget: where ever you go on a holiday, you will ALWAYS meet a Dutch person. Even in rural China…

Steven

#26 WINDMILLS

Apart from those uncomfortable wooden shoes (you know the ones), there is possibly no other Dutch object as iconic as the windmill.

Not surprisingly, the widespread use of the windmill was a result of two very cardinal Dutch traits: practicality and necessity. A lot of wind blows over this flat little country and windmills provided a cheap and efficient power source enabling the Dutch to saw wood planks (for ship building), grind grains, make paper and hammer metals.

The Lowlands have always had one mortal enemy W-A-T-E-R, and water mills served as a crucial tool in battling against the elements. Living in a low country constantly threatened by rising sea levels, the Dutch have always needed to master water control, and *poldermolen* (dike mills) were used to drain fields and move water.

There are around 1000 windmills left in the Lowlands, a far cry from the 10,000+ that used to proliferate the Dutch landscape. These were replaced by mechanical pumping stations in the early 1900s. The remaining windmills are now mostly protected historical monuments. Dutch people have taken their love for *molens* a step further by living in them; 15% of the remaining mills in Holland are currently being used as homes!

As with any country, items that play a significant role in the culture often make their way into the lexicon. Take the numerous Dutch expressions referring to windmills as proof of their importance and enormous cultural significance:

De molen gaat niet om met wind die voorbij is.
Literal translation: The windmill doesn't care about the wind that came before (i.e. don't worry yourself with the past/ the past is the past).

Een klap van de molen gekregen hebben.
Literal translation: Been hit by a windmill (i.e. to describe someone who is irrational/ not making sense).

Dat is koren op zijn molen.
Literal translation: That is grist (ground grain) to his mill (i.e. that which supports/ strengthens his own argument).

Tegen windmolens vechten
Literal translation: To fight with windmills (i.e. to describe the futility of a fight/ to fight a losing battle).

WHAT OUR COMMUNITY HAS TO SAY

The windmills made the Golden Age possible! Some dude was clever enough to hook up a windmill to a saw to produce wooden planks in far greater volumes than could be done by hand. That way it was possible to build a huge amount of ships in a (for that age) very short time.

Michiel

hij loopt met molentjes (he walks with small mills): which means: he is crazy hij draait met alle winden mee: (he turns with all winds): he changes his opinion, depending on the person he talks with alle molens vangen wind (all mills catch wind): each concurrent takes part of the profit

Mieke

Go to Schiedam for the tallest windmills in the world.

Hessel

With the industrial revolution of the late middle ages a lot of mills were built througout Western Europe. In surrounding countries watermills were more prevalent, but although the Netherlands have many streams and rivers, height differences were usually not sufficient to power the typical watermolen. Wind however, passed over this flat country unhindered. As a consequence, windmills sprouted up all over the landscape.

A mill, of course, is just a power source. They can be used to saw planks, manufacture paper from wood or textile pulp, grind grains, hammer steel, and also to move water.
Windmills are found all over Europe in many shapes and sizes. Typical for the Netherlands are the rows of windmills that were build to empty the polders and for water management. Today the water is managed entirely with electrical mills, although a few steam mills remain as functioning museums and as a back up.

Ablabius

#27 PICKING THEIR NOSES

I WAS AT A TRADE FAIR IN ASIA. COMPANIES FROM ALMOST EVERY COUNTRY IN THE WORLD WERE PRESENT SHOWING THEIR LOCAL PRODUCTS FOR EXPORT. A COLLEAGUE AND I WERE MANNING OUR STAND AND TO PASS THE TIME WE DECIDED TO PLAY THE "WHAT-COUNTRY-DO-YOU-THINK-THEY'RE-FROM?" GAME. WE STARTED WITH THE STAND ACROSS THE AISLE.

FOUR TALL BLOND MEN IN COMPANY-BRANDED POLO SHIRTS WERE BUSY ARRANGING THEIR MATERIALS. MY CO-WORKER DECLARED THAT THEY WERE EITHER A) GERMAN, B) DUTCH, OR C) DANISH. WE COLLECTIVELY RULED OUT C) BUT WERE TORN BETWEEN A) AND B). TO MAKE THE GAME MORE INTERESTING I WAGERED A BET OF 20 EUROS AND WE GAVE OURSELVES 5 MORE MINUTES TO STUDY OUR SUBJECTS.

AFTER 5 MINUTES MY FRIEND GAVE UP. I TOO WAS GOING TO CONCEDE. WHEN, ALMOST IN SLOW MOTION – I SAW ONE OF THE MEN'S HANDS SLOWING MAKING ITS WAY TOWARDS HIS FACE. HIS INDEX FINGER WAS HELD ERECT AS IT WAS FORCEFULLY SHOVED INTO HIS LEFT NOSTRIL. "I GOT IT!" I SHOUTED EXCITEDLY – "DUTCH. DUTCH. DUTCH! MY MONEY'S ON DUTCH!!" MY FRIEND WAS SHOCKED BY MY SUDDEN CLARITY. "HE'S PICKING HIS NOSE!" I SQUEALED PROUDLY. "DUTCH MEN PICK THEIR NOSE IN PUBLIC!" WITH A LOOK OF DISBELIEF. MY FRIEND MARCHED OVER TO THEIR BOOTH. STRUCK UP A BRIEF CONVERSATION AND SOON GAVE ME THE THUMBS UP BEHIND HER BACK. SURE ENOUGH. I WAS THE WINNER – THE NOSE-PICKER WAS INDEED DUTCH!

We are happy to be the first to put it out there; Dutch people like to pick their noses. They must like it, because they do it all the time! It is one thing to pick your nose in the privacy of your own home, but Dutchies appear to be quite alright with committing this offense in public and without shame.

The Dutch paper, GezondNU conducted a study in the Netherlands and found that over 90% of Dutch people admit to picking their noses. Moreover, half of the respondents said they did so more than once a day. Even stranger was the fact that nearly 50% of all Dutch people find nose-picking to be "disgusting" when they see others doing it. The study further stated that over a third of Dutch men report that they like to *"...draai er een balletje van en schiet dat weg"* (translation: roll it in a ball and flick it). Make it stop!

We will admit that this appears to be mainly a man-thing. Just take a look around, Dutch men picking their noses can be found everywhere – on the metro, in cars, on bikes, at work – you name it!

The bottom line? Picking your nose in public is gross and barbaric. Don't do it. Not even if the King thinks it is appropriate royal behaviour.

WHAT OUR COMMUNITY HAS TO SAY

I was picking my nose when I read this.

Linda

I absolutely love this! My husband is Dutch and he always does this–nose picking!!!! We would always argue about it but he keeps doing it especially when he is driving the car. Really annoying but now he's doing his best to avoid it (but probably when I'm only with him).

Lei

O. M. G! Sooooo true! I see it everywhere! And indeed, only men… I always have 'plaatsvervangende schaamte' when I see a man digging his way up to his brain…

Sjess

Haa aaaahahahahahah ahahaahahahahahahaah ahahahaahahahhahahahaaaah ahahahahahahahahahahahahaha haha I CAN'T STOP LAUGHING IT'S SO TRUE! And we love our King for it Sign of being a real human, not some trained pet.

Steffen

Perhaps I've just been lucky not to come accross any. I got to know a Dutchman very well over a couple of years and never once saw him pick his nose. I also visited Holland (staying in The Hague) last year and didn't see any. I found them to be all very polite so perhaps it depends on what crowd you mix with..

Mandy

Nose-picking is lovely. It is masturbation!

Roland

I was on train from Schiphol to Amsterdam a couple years ago and watched the woman in front of me (in a business suit), pick her nose, examine it and then wipe it down the back of the seat in front of her. Another time, also on the train, I watched a man pick his nose, examine it, EAT it and then repeat with his earwax. His chewing was so loud and smacking that I had to crank up the music in my headphones. You didn't mention the snot eating in your post, it needs to be mentioned. Also, one of the reasons why my bare hands never touch doorknobs, taps or handrails – always with a sleeve or a tissue.

amansterdama

At least twice in Holland I've been admiring an attractive girl in the next car, and then she's started picking her nose, and then eaten it. I find it amazing how the attraction evaporates!

swhite44

Thanks. Now I'm officially ashamed of being Dutch. This and the red pants thing. Wait. I'm not... It does sound awful familiar though.

Steven

PFFF! That is SO true. I'm a Dutch gal and I had a boyfriend who did that all the time, I told him how disgusting it was to do anywhere near me and in public. His only reply was: "What? It's only natural".

Mila

It's predominantly done by men because they have bigger noses. :-P
Way back – before paper tissues were invented – the Dutch always had a kerchief handy. But in every country they conquered, the inhabitants used to make fun of their snot being so precious that they wrapped it in a cloth and carried it around, so they abolished the practice.
(And blowing your nose is bad for the brain – or was it the ear-drums – because of the high pressure in the cavities.)

Ablabius

#28 FRIES AND MAYO

Call them what you will – *friet, friets, patat, Vlaamse Frieten* – but one thing is for sure, the Dutch can't seem to get enough of them! In fact, they love 'em so much that they eat over 41 million kilos of these bad boys per year! We wouldn't want your brains to explode, so we'll kindly do the maths for you; that equals 2.5 kilos (5.5 lbs) of fries per Dutchie per year! Oh my…

In English we refer to them as French Fries, but the French can't take claim for this invention. Sadly, neither can the Dutch. Fries, in fact, originated from the Dutch people's favourite neighbour, Belgium. It is believed that they were named "french fries" by American WW1 soldiers who were stationed there. They called the Belgian fries "French" as this was the official language of the Belgian army at that time.

Fries were common place in Belgium as early as 1680 but didn't reach the Lowlands until the early 1900s. In 1912, the first *patat-friet* house popped up in Rotterdam's red light district.

What makes Dutch fries so different? The toppings, my friends, the toppings! Did you not see the now infamous scene in Pulp Fiction?

Yes, mayo is the *friets'* best friend in the lowlands. The two share a beautiful romance and can be found together all over town. Sometimes mayo's cheaper cousin, *frietsaus*, makes an appearance with its unknown ingredients, but for the most part friets and mayo go hand in hand.

Refer to our cheat-sheet below if you want to impress folks with your knowledge of these uniquely Dutch toppings and sauces:

- *Friet met satésaus*: fries with peanut sauce
- *Friet speciaal*: fries with mayonnaise, (curry) ketchup and onions
- *Patatje Joppie*: fries with the "top-secret" Joppiesaus (actually just a mixture of mayonnaise, ketchup and spices)
- *Patatje oorlog:* this varies slightly by region but is often served as fries with peanut sauce, mayonnaise and raw chopped onions. Oorlog, the Dutch word for war, is a reference to the sloppy mess this dish entails
- *Kapsalon:* fries with kebab or shawarma and sometimes cheese

WHAT OUR COMMUNITY HAS TO SAY

Patatje oorlog, in the south of the Netherlands we eat it with Mayonaise, Ketchup, chopped raw onions and sate sauce, yum yum, i miss it!

Sandra

As a dutch woman living in America, I always request a side of mayonaise with my fries at restaurants. They either look at me like I'm crazy or ask if I'm from Holland. The mayonaise is not like what we get in Holland but sometimes it gets pretty close. I always have an imported stash of mayonaise and curry in my pantry. It is the fee my family and fries are required to pay when they come to visit from the Netherlands. That and douwe egberts coffee, honing wybertjes, gehakt en kip kruiden and anything salmiak…
… Excuse me while I go raid my stash. You've made me homesick!

Joyce

I still eat my fries with mayo after 21 years in the US.

Florence

My boyfriend from the USA still thinks it is strange if I, Dutchie, talk about fries as a dinner. For my boyfriend fries are not a meal, but a side dish. But I can eat just one frietje speciaal and that would be my dinner. If I am hungry, I might take a snack to go with it

Kate

I never thought mayo and fries would be a good combination till I tried Friet speciaal a few months back when I was in Breda… absolutely divine!

Mariah

friet with curry ketchup! yes, now I'm craving it

Dutch mayonaise is different from French or some German brands, because they use (more) vinegar whereas 'we' use oil. It makes the mayonaise thicker and less fresh/sour (but the downside is the calories intake). This is why you see Dutch families taking their own jars of mayonaise with them on holidays.

Jasper

Being a Dutchie living in Italy, one of the things I have to eat within three days after my arrival in Holland is a Frietje Speciaal! After my stay, I will always, just always bring some mayonnaise and curry in my suitcase. Risky, I have ruined some clothes when the jar broke during traveling….

Mina

#29 LIQUORICE

Dutch people love liquorice. This may not seem particularly strange, but let it be known that this liquorice is not the kind you are most likely accustomed to. Dutch liquorice is not at all similar to the North American variety of red spiral sticks or the slightly-salty black chewy stuff. The Dutch prefer a much stronger version which in polite terms can be referred to as "medicinal", and in more direct terms can be described as "poison"!

Proof of their penchant; Dutch people eat the most liquorice per capita than any other people in the world!

The Dutch *drop* (liquorice) comes in a variety of different flavours and genres. There are four primary types of *drop*:
· soft & sweet   · hard & sweet
· soft & salty   · hard & salty

Don't let the word "sweet" or "soft" fool you though, none of the above taste like they sound.

Drop can be bought just about anywhere, but can also be found in drugstores and pharmacies as Dutch people believe that it also has some medicinal properties (mainly concerning sore throats and tummy aches).

Drop doesn't come in spirally tubes or sticks like it does across the pond, but rather interesting shapes such as circles, squares, diamonds, ovals, cubes and coins. A new trend appears to be theme-shaped *drop*. Love cars? Try some tasty *Autodrop*. Like cats? (So much that you might want to eat them?) Well, then you're sure to love *Katjes drop*!

DUTCH PEOPLE EAT MORE THAN 4 POUNDS OF LIQUORICE PER PERSON, PER YEAR

The pinnacle of foul-tasting Dutch liquorice is the very scary *Dubbel Zout* (double salt) variety. Non-Dutch have been known to contort their faces into the strangest of expressions when attempting to try this Dutch treat. Many a foreigner has had no choice but to promptly spit out the stuff at first taste. We recommend you try it at your peril!

WHAT OUR COMMUNITY HAS TO SAY

I live in Grand Rapids, Michigan, and worked in Holland, Michigan. Since we have so many people of Dutch descent in West Michigan, Dubbel Zout is not hard to find, though if the laws were just it would be. Oh, that is terrible, terrible stuff that should not be considered food or medicine! Chocolate on bread for breakfast, that's fine, but please do not try to pass off Dubbel Zout as licorice!

Walt

This article made me hungry! I'm going to get myself a dropje!

tGiel

I -LOVE- Dubbel Zout. My dad and sister can't eat it, (she got frenchie taste buds from him) but mom and I went through it at a rate of a couple pounds a month back when we lived near a candy store that carried it in the states. Soooo good. Now I'm totally craving DZ drop and hagelslag. Darn you, I'll never find either of those things where I live now.

I seriously just can NOT understand that anyone would NOT like 'our' drop? It's delicious! I eat kilos of that stuff, especially autodrop. And not to forget the 'katjes' drop (yes, drop shaped like cats). That tube shaped spirally stuff in the English drop doesn't even come close to dutch drop!

Twansparant

When I went to America for a new job I started off with an orientation week with a group of people from all over the world. Being Dutch I am not able to live without licorice, especially not without the dubbel zoute. So I brought enough with me to survive for a while .When we were asked to tell something about our country I decided to let my new foreign friends try out some of my dubbel zoute licorice. Their faces were hilarious and I believe none of them actually finished eating the licorice. They could not believe we call it candy, and actually enjoy eating it. It was a hard year for me since Dutch licorice is hard to find in the USA

Martine

Dutch licorice is horrible. I am 3rd generation Dutch immigrant and my Grandparents love that stuff. The best thing ever was when my grandpa (with the egging on of my father) tricked my poor southern born and raised, fried cornbread eating, banana pudding loving husband into eating this "candy." Lets just say I warned him…

Janna

Love droppies…all sizes, colors, shapes and flavours!!! Reading this blog is making my mouth water and I'm seriously considering driving by the Dutch deli to get some on the way home. I also have enjoyed getting my Canadian friends to try it. It's actually kind of disappointing when they like it!! My favourite is the "brown bears" and when feeling like a challenge there is always the triple-salted droppies!! Yum, yum and yum!!!

Next vacation, don't forget to bring loads of drop and see how many foreigners will puke

Bernjan

Lisa

#30 FORCING DROP ON UNSUSPECTING FOREIGNERS

Dutch people have yet another liquorice-related love: forcing *drop* onto unsuspecting foreigners.

We can only assume this behaviour is some sort of Dutch taste-bud-superiority-test or perhaps a way of testing how Dutch someone is (or has the potential to become).

Dutch people get a serious kick out of watching non-Dutch people grimace while sucking on their beloved *drop*. A quick search on the internet will lead to an even more disturbing trend; Dutch people feeding *drop* to non-Dutch people and recording it. Their victims span the globe (Americans, Brits, Japanese, you name it), and they are relentless in their torturous crimes. The next time an innocent Dutch person offers you "a candy", remember you have been warned!

DESPERATELY
SEEKING AN INTERPRETER

WHAT AN ANGLOPHONE SAYS	WHAT AN ANGLOPHONE MEANS	WHAT A DUTCH PERSON UNDERSTANDS
How are you?	Hello	He wants to know exactly how I am feeling and I have to give an accurate and truthful answer
Correct me if I'm wrong	I know I'm right, but	She is unsure of what she is saying
That's not bad	That's quite good to very good	That's mediocre at best
Perhaps you would like to think about...	I would really suggest you think about this	A suggestion but I can do what I like
I was a bit disappointed that	I am quite upset with you	Not really important
Please think about that some more	Bad idea, I urge you to reconsider	They like the idea!
That's interesting	I might be mildly interested	They're impressed
You must come for dinner sometime	Just being polite (not an invitation)	I will receive an invitation very soon
That is an original point of view	You're just silly	They like my ideas!
I hear you	I agree with you	Not sure if she agrees or not
IMHO (=in my humble opinion)	I'm not really humble and you're wrong	He's unsure of his position

#31 KEEPING IT REAL

The Dutch are big fans of authenticity and take pride in the genuine. In short, they like to keep it real. This behaviour is closely related to the Calvinist "doe normaal" attitude and is often used to justify Dutch people's infamous directness.

Speak to any Dutch person after they have returned from a trip to America and they are sure to mention "American fakeness" in their travel tales. The Dutch are allergic to the American "good-morning-how-y'all-doing" lingo. They shudder when entering an American store, only to be greeted by those five annoying little words: "How are you doing today?" It's a fairly innocent question for North Americans or Brits, but for the Dutch it is downright scandalous. "Why are they asking?", "Why do they care?", "They don't even wait for my answer!" The Dutch are a reticent bunch and overt American-type friendliness is so foreign to them that it's downright offensive.

Of course the teenage girl folding sweaters in the Gap doesn't really care how you are doing. Of course the waitress serving you fries isn't actually asking to hear about your awful day. What the Dutch don't seem to understand is that the asking of "How are you" is a gesture of friendliness rather than a formal inquisition into the state of your mental well-being.

The Dutch could in fact learn a thing or two from the American "customer is king" attitude. It is a well-known fact that Dutch customer service is a bit rough around the edges. American comedian Seth Meyers summed it up best, *"When I was [in Amsterdam], people's big complaint about America was that the waitresses were fake-nice. In Amsterdam, you know, the waiters generally fucking hate you."* Hmmm… which do you prefer?

WHAT OUR COMMUNITY HAS TO SAY

Well I think most Dutch just do not understand that the phrase 'How are you' is more the equivalent of the Dutch 'Goedemiddag' (Good Afternoon). And I totally agree that the service in horrible in many places.

Ron

Being Dutch myself, I still don't know how to deal with the "Hi, how are ya?" It's not an automated process for me and it still catches me off guard wanting to give a sincere answer. I guess it clashes with our "Dutch sincerity/directness" I.e. if you're not really interested why ask me how I am? Or what business of yours is it how I am today, stranger?

Michael

Agreed, a 'hey, how are you?' is generally a question I only ask to people (friends) when I'm actually curious for the answer. To be asked such a (personal/private) question out of context just makes you feel awkward even when you know its custom in another culture.

Jasper

I'm from the Netherlands and I can confirm that it is true that we don't like it if people say 'how are you?' instead of hello without wanting to know the answer.... But that every waiter in Amsterdam fucking hates you? Not too sure about that. And I think in generals waiters are not that friendly in cities that are flooded by tourists.

Mar

I live in Groningen; waiters here are rude and we do not get many tourists. It's a Dutch thing.

Stacey

Interesting. I agree: I hate 'fakeness' as well...but I also think that in Holland not only waiters can be more polite and sometimes I don't even get a 'thank you' or a 'hello' in shops anymore. So I guess I don't like a question when I'm entering a store of café, but a 'goodmorning' with a smile would be most welcome.

Priscilla

The thing is,"How are you this morning?" is just rhetorical. But initially, as a foreigner, you don't hear this, and the Dutch being rather literal-minded, misinterpret it and think they're actually being asked about their state of health and mind. They're not.

Miss Footloose

As a Dutch person living in Texas, I love the 'fakeness', which is not always fake. Whenever I visit Holland, I can't believe how rude people are! I love having conversations with strangers in stores And for those Dutchies who don't know what to say when someone asks "How are you doing today?", just reply "I'm fine, how are you?" and move on.

dutchgirlintexas77

Love your blog! Always makes me laugh. I'm a Dutch living in Canada and your blog really helps me explain myself to my Quebecois friends and colleagues. Yes, we are very direct people, but I don't agree on Dutch waiters and supermarket employees being rude, at least not in the smaller cities and villages. If I compare it to the waiters here in Montreal the Dutch are extremely friendly!

Sanne

I am Dutch, and prefer to be greeted when I enter a shop, I hate it when I enter or leave a shop and no one has acknowledged me... What I do hate is when shop attendants swoop on you when you just want to browse, and never let you out of their sights (it's what Dutch sales people do very well!).As far as that's concerned, I actually prefer the American way of being proud of what you do, and not being seen as a failure when something doesn't work out the way you wanted it to. I think I'm living in the wrong country for the kind of person I am...

Desirée

Well... Agree with the first part but not every dutch waiter is that way. I live in the hague and service is the worst in amsterdam. Especially in hip and happening places.

Floor

I don't think 'the dutch' as a whole compared to any other group of people from any other country are more grumpy nor happy. It's just a traditional thing, usually to do with the way you were raised by your parents. And yes, I do get a little miffed when someone who doesn't care at all how my day is insists on asking about it anyway. Now I realize they don't literally mean to inquire about your day but it is just how we dutchies interpret a greeting like that. Probably because over here a simple 'good day sir' or ma'am will do just fine.

Tom

I'm Dutch and I regularly work with US tourists. I think I can say about myself I'm polite and professional (hey, I've come a long way, so it seems!). But the fakeness that goes around there I often cannot handle. When you ask them a genuine "all fine?" and you get the standard "oh it's great" answer you have no idea what's going on. It happened that all happy smily people write complaint emails to my boss afterwards. How the hell are you supposed to improve your service when you never really know what they think? So I much prefer the Dutch way – if it's not good, you can read their faces, ask them a direct question, get a direct honest answer and solve the problem.

Liz

#32 NAMES THAT SOUND RIDICULOUS IN ENGLISH

If you live in the Lowlands long enough, you may eventually have to compose an email that starts with the phrase "Dear Joke" or better yet, "Hello Freek". We can assure you that you will have difficulty keeping a straight face when introducing your friend Floor to your friend Taco. The reality is that most Dutch names sound ridiculous in English. You may have seen the Fokkers on the silver screen but you probably didn't know that the Netherlands is full of Fokkers!

Names like Door, Harm, and Kok are all sure to produce quizzical looks or giggles from English speaking folks. Thinking of having a child with international prospects? We would suggest avoiding names that starts with a "J". Jaap, Jarno, Joost and Joop, and their good friends Jurgen, Joord and Jelle aren't going to have an easy time explaining how to pronounce their names outside of the Lowlands.

Let's take a moment to address the poor Dutch child that grows up in the farming fields of Friesland, and decides to spread their wings and start a life in an Anglophone country, named: Aad van de Vaart. Yes, we won't blame you if you giggle like a schoolgirl every time you hear that last name (Vaart is pronounced similar to the English word "fart"). Call us juvenile, but that name is sure to get a lot of laughs in the school yard!

The top tongue-twister are those names of Friesian origin that start with "Sj". If you're lucky, you won't ever have the misfortune of having to read any of these names aloud:

BOYS :				
	SJAAK	SJAN	SJENG	SJOMALI
	SJACO	SJASTRA	SJIMMIE	SJORS
	SJAKIE	SJEF	SJINKI	SJORSJE
	SJAKKO	SJEI	SJOERD	SJUUL
	SJAM			

GIRLS :				
	SJAHCANDRA	SJANIEKE	SJARLOT	SJORSJE
	SJAMANA	SJANIEN	SJASTRA	SJOUKE
	SJAN	SJANOEK	SJEL	SJOUKJE
	SJANETTE	SJARLIE	SJORA	SJUULKE

Names like these might work very well in the Lowlands, but something is definitely lost in translation. Huh? Your Dutch parents named you what?!?

All of this may be terribly amusing to non-Dutch people, but to be honest, there are many Dutch names that are equally ridiculous even in Dutch! How else would one explain Meneer Zonderkop (Mr. Without Head) or Mevrouw Naaktgeboren (Mrs. Born Naked)? And how about the innocent child blessed with the last name Niemandsvriend (nobody's friend). Let's just hope his parents didn't name him Sicco.

LOST IN TRANSLATION :

Fokje Modder

Dick de Kok

Naaktgeboren (born naked)

Zonderbroek (without pants)

Pannekoek (pancake)

Aarsman (assman)

Zonderkop (without head)

Tiny Kox (Dutch politician)

Nijs Kok

Wierd Duk (Journalist)

Robin Hoedjes

Bennie Dood (I'm not dead)

WHAT OUR COMMUNITY HAS TO SAY

Hey if you wondering about those silly surnames (Naaktgeboren, Poepjes (Poopies), Holvast (Assgrip) Klootwijk (Village of Balls). In the time that Napoleon ruled the Netherlands a lot of Dutch didnt really have a last name or something like the son of name (Klaaszoon, Janzoon) So every Dutchy was obliged to pick a surname and register it. A lot of us didnt take it seriously and took the most silly names to screw with Napoleon or they thought it would all blow over. Haha but it didnt.

Gido

Well apparently that is really more of a very widespread myth. Most dutchies already had a proper surname by then, although not necessarily registered anywhere, or written down in any way. The Napoleon thing mostly just caused spellings to become fixed. Many of the surnames are more like degenerations of previous surnames, for example: nageboren slowly turning into naaktgeboren, or baerst slowly turning into borst.

Rood

This is not totally true. Many people in the southern en western parts of the Netherlands did have surnames before Napoleon ruled. Most people in the northern parts did not have surnames. Those who did have surnames were mostly wealthier or "immigrants" from Germany, France or the southern or western parts of the Netherlands.

Jiske

My fav is Zonderbroek – without trousers.

whowants tolickthespoon

Ha ha! My daughter married a Kok! However, her husband's parents chose to pronounce it as "Cook". So of course she says "Cook" but always has to spell it as K O K.

Margaret

Back in the days, we had a Prime Minister by the name of Wim Kok. he once headed a trade delegation to the far East (China, Japan) and was accompanied by a whole bunch of people, including various captains of industry, including the CEO of KPN (the incumbent telecom operator), named Wim Dik. I can only imagine the looks on the faces of the hosts when being introduced…..

DJ

Lol, you made me laugh… I am one of those with a problem name. I'm called Joke and live in England……. I refuse to change my name, but in official circumstances I use my official name Johanna. With friends I'll always be Joke, even if that causes giggles sometimes. At least we've got a subject to talk about… But when I started my first job in the UK, I had to use Johanna since my e-mail address would work out as joke@companyname.org.uk….. Not exactly good promotion for the company….I believe every culture and language has funny names though, but I've made sure that my son has a name that works in most languages

Joke

My uncle worked for a wheelchair business called Beenhakker (Legchopper). Not joking!

Gido

I remember living in the US, when Wim Dik and Wim Kok came to visit on a financial delegation trip.

Nicky

Don't forget the famous American actor Dick van Dijk.

Marjolein

Jeroen

I knew a guy named Dick Kok.

Floor

Had a chuckle reading this... My name is Floor and I went to an international school all my life. So I am used to the 'ceiling' jokes, 'letting people walk all over me' etc etc. When I decided people could also call me Flora in the UK I was unaware there was a margarine brand with that name. I then got comments like 'You must spread easy'. Ah well, at least I didn't have to keep spelling it. Back in Holland I'm almost disappointed my name isn't strange anymore. Great blog!

Danny

My son is called Jeroen and most English speaking people that do not know the name pronounce it as urine. Not so funny when you're 12 years old, but we have many laughs about it

Rutger

Try to pronounce Rutger the Dutch way, it's impossible if you're not Dutch.

Edu

And why exactly do Dutch have to sound right in English? It's DUTCH for people in the NETHERLANDS. They speak a different language there, with different habits and different names. As if there aren't any silly names here in England (I'm Dutch, moved to the UK) that sound utterly ridiculous in English or in Dutch. Dutch people did not and do not chose names to piss other people (the English) off. Maybe Napoleon (as mentioned earlier) but he's French. And hey, don't we all love to piss the French off a bit?

Fanny

All of this is so recognisable! I lived in the states for a short time, where I encountered some memorable responses to my name. Ranging from "that's so funny" (or grappig, as many Dutch people kindly nickname me) to "that's such a good joke! Now what's your real name?" What can I say. Thanks mummy and daddy for calling me Fanny Bot?

Ann

So change your name in foreign countries. Why be a mockery? I'll NEVER comprehend why people insist on shoving their names down other culture's throats when they know it's offensive. You CAN change your name, you know. You might consider calling yourself 'buttocks', same meaning. Why burden yourself as a joke? Short of that, stay home where they don't mind.

#33 KING'S DAY
(FORMERLY KNOW AS QUEEN'S DAY)

For a nation which often prides itself on "normal" behaviour and following the rules, King's Day is truly nothing of the sort. It's the one day of the year where the Dutch break all their self-imposed rules and let loose in a way that puts all other nations to shame. To say that King's Day is the world's greatest party is nothing short of an understatement. Simply put: King's Day is epic.

Koningsdag (King's Day) is celebrated on the 27th of April – King Willem's birthday. It's celebrated throughout the entire country, with over 1 million visitors joining Amsterdam's 1 million residents in a city-wide street party. During this *oranjegekte* (orange-crazed) day Dutch people hawk their household wares on the streets, tax free, turning entire Dutch cities into lively flea-markets.

If you haven't experienced the pure joviality and joy of a city flooded in Orange, I dare say you haven't truly lived. Bells sound, bands play, children perform, deals are made, bargains are found, drinks are consumed, and above all, love, laughter and smiles abound.

For a nation often divided, King's Day is the great equaliser. Unlike other countries' national days, April 27th is not about in-your-face patriotism or royal worshipping. It's about oneness: everyone can partake, everyone can celebrate, and everyone can belong. So come 27 April, throw on an orange t-shirt, join the crowds and party like a Dutchie!

I MUST SAY THAT KONINGSDAG DOESN'T QUITE ROLL OFF THE TONGUE AS NICELY AS THE FORMER KONINGINNEDAG DID. I PRACTICED MY PRONUNCIATION FOR YEARS – AND ONCE I FINALLY MASTERED IT, THE QUEEN UP AND DECIDED TO ABDICATE! GO FIGURE. HOW ELSE CAN FOREIGNERS IMPRESS DUTCHIES WITH OUR SKILFUL PRONUNCIATIONS? I SUPPOSE IT'S BACK TO SCHEVENINGEN AS THE SHIBBOLETH OF CHOICE!

WHAT OUR COMMUNITY HAS TO SAY

What you've missed here is the look on all the faces of those tourists that are in Amsterdam on Queens-day purely by accident, and who have the total shock and horror engraved upon their faces. It's so much fun to see a 60 year old woman form Cleveland Ohio thinking:
"I knew Europe was a cesspool, but that this was as bad as this????"

xe0104

A totally true story, love the way you write about us Dutchies…

Yvonne

I live in Amsterdam but I hate Queensday. All these drunk loud obnoxious people, trash all over the place, people shoving you.. YUCK! Gaypride is such a better event in Amsterdam, less obnoxious and drunk people, better atmosphere in the city!

Adriana

Hahahahaha…
I'm laughing so hard here! Perfect description! But indeed you forgot to mention about the boats and the "Pee" stands… I was so surprised to see every guy just putting their "boy" out of their pants and going right there in the middle of the fun! No door, no privacy, no shame!! Four stands in one! I had to take a picture of my husband last year! Nobody would ever believed me!!!

Rosana

Queensday on a boat, in the sun, music, beer, orange paint all over your face, drunk, tired, dancing, people watching, a collection of 50 cents coins in your pocket to pay for the toilet at bar for the toilet lady (also typical Dutch?), preparing your orange outfit a month ahead as it can't be the same as the year before! It also seems that it is for some reason, ALWAYS sunny on queensday!

Femke

First of all I love your posts about your "adoptive country" !! Truly insight for foreigners AND dutchies about our little country soon to be colored Orange to celebrate OUR national holiday.Dutchies all over the world though do their little bit (or little bigger bit) to bring the color Orange beyond their borders. As a dutchie in the USA, I'll be going to a Queensday party here, but there are plenty of parties all over the world. I've counted over 50 so far and but am pretty sure there are "one or two" more …. Just take a look and maybe there is a Queensday party near you !!!Have fun everybody !!!

Laura

#34 DAT KAN NIET

If you arrive in the Lowlands speaking very little Dutch, you will quickly pick up on a few essential phrases. One of Dutch people's favourite phrases is *"Dat kan niet"*, essentially translating to a simple but curt, *"That cannot be done"*. An even more annoying version is *"Dat mag niet"*, which manifests into the more assertive and dictating, *"That may not be done"*. Uses for both are endless but they are most often employed as a conversation killer, for instance:

"I need my internet fixed this week."
"Dat kan niet".
End of conversation.

"I would like to have no mayonnaise on my sandwich, please"
"Dat kan niet".
End of conversation.

"Can I pay with a credit card?"
"Dat mag niet".
End of conversation.

The beauty of these phrases is that you really can't argue with them. *"Dat kan niet"* and *"Dat mag niet"* have an unfair advantage and always seems to win. This explains their resounding popularity in the Dutch customer service/un-service field.

How many times a day are Dutch people simultaneously uttering those 3 highly irritating words? We'll take a shot – 16 million – an average of one "Dat kan niet" per person, per day! (That should make up for the UPC televisie guy who said it 12 times yesterday!)

A close second for most common Dutch phrase is *"Het is niet mogelijk"* – which is essentially just another way of telling you in Dutch that you "ain't going to get what you want". Het is niet mogelijk (actual translation; It is not possible!) pops up at the most inopportune times. It is often just when you thought you were making progress (while changing your mobile phone plan, negotiating with your landlord, or ordering a meal modification) that *"Het is niet mogelijk"*, will rear its ugly little head.

If you plan on working in a customer related environment and would like to give true Dutch service, it is recommended you make use of these phrases at least once in each customer interaction. We hope you have been sufficiently informed, as we will not be repeating these instructions – after all, *"Het is niet mogelijk!"*

THE OTHER DAY I HEARD TWO DUTCH 3 YEAR-OLDS PLAYING IN THE PARK. ONE WAS YELLING "DAT KAN NIET!" AND THE OTHER WAS YELLING BACK "DAT KAN WEL!" THEIR EXCHANGE WENT BACK AND FORTH FOR QUITE SOME TIME. ONLY TO GET LOUDER AND LOUDER: DAT KAN NIET. DAT KAN WEL. DAT KAN NIET!! DAT KAN WEL!!" I STOPPED AND JOINED IN THE FUN. AND BOY IT FELT GRAND! AS I WALKED AWAY I HAD TO WONDER: IF 3 YEAR-OLDS ARE ALREADY BUSY FEVERISHLY PRACTICING AND PERFECTING THEIR FAVOURITE PHRASES. WHAT HOPE DO WE HAVE?!}

WHAT OUR COMMUNITY HAS TO SAY

What about "Dat mag je niet doen," or the even worse, more rude more make me want to slap them across the face "dat mag je ECHT niet doen." I had e neighbor tell me "dat mag je ECHT niet doen" in regards to having an argument with my ex. What is it with Dutch people trying to tell you how you may or may not live your private life in your own house?

Sabrina

i vaguely remember having arguments at the age of 4 that went something like this:"Dat mag niet!""'t mag wel""Niet""Wel""NIET DUS!""WEL HOOR!" and so on.

Quirine

after 7 years in NL, i moved away. on my first visit back, it took a whole 15 mins before someone uttered that familiar phrase, at the AKO shop at schiphol. i can't remember what was in question, but clearly, 'dat kan niet.' good to be back!

Sunburn

The real popular (and annoying) one is: "Dat is niet de bedoeling", literally "that is not intended", but is actually a mild way of saying "you are not supposed to do that!" without spelling it out.

Arjen

So I started reading this maybe 2 months before moving to Amsterdam, today (my second day) I encountered the "Dat kan nie" phrase, although it was inconviencing me, I really laughed at the accuracy and how predictable dutch can be

Alphiwe

The one phrase i really cant stand is 'regels zijn regels', which in general also means that there is a better way to do things, but that person simply refuses to even consider them because the rules say 'dat kan niet'. Even when the rules are clearly stupid and dont seem to work well with the situation at all, theyre preferred to just thinking outside the box a little bit and avoiding a lot of unnecessary fuss.

M

127

#35 IMPOSSIBLY STEEP STAIRS

AFTER 2 YEARS OF LIVING IN THE LOWLANDS OUR EXPAT-PROVIDED ACCOMMODATION RAN OUT. SO WE NAIVELY EMBARKED ON AN AMSTERDAM HOUSE-HUNTING MISSION. THE WHOLE PROCESS FELT A BIT LIKE THE STORY OF "THE THREE BEARS": TOO SMALL, TOO BIG, TOO HARD, TOO SOFT – YOU GET THE IDEA.

POTENTIAL APARTMENT #34 WAS ONE OF MY FAVOURITES. LOCATED ON A PICTURESQUE AMSTERDAM CANAL – IT WAS LIKE STEPPING INTO A POSTCARD. TRUE IT WAS COSY (READ: INCREDIBLY SMALL), SLIGHTLY DAMP (READ: MAJOR WATER LEAKAGE THROUGHOUT THE HOUSE), AND AMBITIOUS (READ: INCONVENIENTLY SPREAD OUT ACROSS 3 TINY LEVELS), BUT IT FIT MY NEW-IN-AMSTERDAM ROMANTICISM AND HOME-FINDING DESPERATION WELL.

I COULD DEAL WITH ALL ITS QUIRKS BUT ITS CRITICAL DOWNFALL THAT I COULDN'T QUITE COME TO TERMS. WITH WAS THE STAIRS! THEY RESEMBLED A COMICAL LADDER OF SORTS THAT REQUIRED A SERIOUS FITNESS LEVEL AND SEVERE CONCENTRATION. IT WAS A CHALLENGE TO GET MYSELF UP THOSE STAIRS. LET ALONE ANY GROCERIES! NEEDLESS TO SAY. WE DIDN'T END UP OF TAKING THE CANAL VIEW APARTMENT. I FIGURED I JUST DIDN'T HAVE THE DUTCH "BALANCING-CIRCUS-ACT" QUALITIES REQUIRED FOR SUCH A DAILY FEAT. WE LUCKILY SETTLED ON APARTMENT #35 – WHERE WE'VE HAPPILY RESIDED (WITH THE DUTCH LUXURY OF AN ELEVATOR) FOR THE LAST 6 YEARS!

The Dutch are masters of treacherously steep stairs. Dutch stairs mimic vertical mountainsides and require gruelling daily scales. The ladder-like contraptions often require the use of all fours and ninja-like balance.

Dutch stairs are often accompanied by a ceiling full of precariously dangling bicycles and strollers roped up on some hand-made elaborate rigging system. A great example of Dutch ingenuity, but a highly disturbing sight if you begin to contemplate the possibility of a single rope snapping.

The trek upwards on these stairwells is no doubt a mission, but the trek downwards is where things start to get interesting. Not only are you dealing with an impossibly steep descent, but the teeny-tiny stair boards often don't even allow for a full footstep (especially a Dutch one), and thus must be manoeuvred in an awkward sidewise motion. Sometimes, for fun, sneaky Dutch architects decide to throw in a curve, adding yet another element of danger. It is no wonder the Dutch word for stairs is *trap*. How aptly named, for they are a trap indeed, of the death-trap variety!!

These terrifying staircases are characteristic of the 17th-century canal houses built throughout the Netherlands. Were the ancient Dutch some sort of circus-performers? Did they have especially tiny feet, very strong legs and a cruel sense of humour? The answer, unfortunately, is rather pedestrian. Historically, canal houses were taxed only on their width; the wider your house, the more taxes you paid. How could a clever Dutchie circumvent a hefty tax bill? Easy: build yourself a very tall, very skinny house which requires a crazy-ass set of stairs. If you dare to venture up a Dutch staircase, remember, you have been warned!

WHAT OUR COMMUNITY HAS TO SAY

Those steep and narrow stairs in Dutch houses are indeed a menace if you don't grow up with them. If you do, you just race up and down them with learned brain-body athleticism

Footloose

Everyone that comes to my place complains about the narrow staircase! And they are Dutch but have lived in post war housing all their lives!

Nina

My Australian (ex) mom-in-law fell down the stairs in my house – she was so not accustomed to stairs in the first place (90% of the houses in Australia are one level) and then the steep stairs curvy stairs here in a normal (!) Dutch rental house.

loved those stairs as a kid, slided down a couple on a matras, it was AWESOME!

I must say that my partner (Dutch one) fall from one of them and broke his leg!

Sacha

Rick

daquiprai

I live in the Eindhoven area. Our stairs are only tolerable for me because of the railing and they are spiral, and therefore a full foot width on the very outside edge (which is where I walk). Even so, I fell down them the second week we lived here, and then we added 'tread grip tape' to the edges.

Meredith

They're insane, aren't they? My great-aunt lives in an ancient house in The Hague, and the stairs are more like a ladder. She is 80+, and not very agile any more – dreading the day that she misjudges the stairs...

Ruth

Did the up and down running for 21 years. 5 floors. Then I moved to the US. I miss them, they keep you fit and trim!

Anja

They seem like a very good, if scary, workout!

Margarita

LOL, I remember taking off my heels and throwing them down before me after which I climbed the stairs down as a ladder on all fours with my socks only :) Once down 3 floors I would put my shoes on again. This was at a friend's house in Amsterdam center. The real challenge was the evenings when I had a little too much to drink

Demmy

I have one of these..and secretly enjoy in anticipation the look on visitor's faces when they enter my apartment. Not in Amsterdam, but Gouda has it's share of 'death traps' as well.

Mike

After 4 years with death trap stairs in our house in Breda I can now run up them carrying a 3 year old under one arm and a basketful of laundry in the other hand (because, of course, the washing machine is in the attic). Still can't cycle while texting though – epic failure as a wannabe Dutchie!

Erica

That blog is the funniest ever! It made me cry !!Dutch people should hire Canadian Architects and live normally without making unwanted backflips-triple-axel figures when going down the stairs.

MJ

131

#36 SINTERKLAAS

You've seen the imagery all over town, that old dude with long white hair and the big pointy red hat. You also know those pesky black-faced fellas he hangs out with, the ones who've whipped pepernoten at your head. You've joined in the heated Zwarte Piet debate, and you've eaten your chocolate initial at work. BUT what really is the deal with this whole Sinterklaas thing?

Basically, all you need to know is that Sinterklaas is the most beloved of all Dutch traditions and holidays. And one that Dutch people are fiercely proud of. Don't you dare go messing about with this very gezellig affair! Check out our handy guide below to help you survive the madness.

Everything you need to know about Sinterklaas:

Q: Where does this old dude and his black-faced friends come from?

A: Sinterklaas is said to have originated from St. Nicolaus, the Bishop of Mira, who lived in Turkey in the 3rd century. According to the legend, he saved the town from starvation, revived a couple of dead children and offered gifts of dowries to poor girls so they didn't have to become prostitutes. Hence, a pretty saintly dude.

Q: How does he get to the lowlands?

A: Nowadays, he sails in from Spain on a ship in late November and rides about town on a white stallion named Amerigo (don't ask) with a handful of energetic black-faced friends who throw things at people.

Q: Huh? Who are these black guys? Elves? Bodyguards?

A: These my friends, are Zwarte Piets, Sint's mischievous helpers and they can be seen everywhere about town violently whipping hard-stone like cookies (aka: pepernoten) at children and passersby. Duck!

SANTA KLAUS VS SINTERKLAAS

A quick guide on the main differences between good old Santa and the Dutch Sinterklaas

	SANTA CLAUS	SINTERKLAAS
Appearance	Casual red & white outfit	Formal church attire
Character	Jovial, friendly, joyful, punctual	Elderly, stately, serious, almost senile at times (needs his Pieten often to remind him of things)
Physical condition	Old, very overweight, slight drinking problem?	Old, but lean & fit
Home	North pole	Spain
Family	Mrs. Claus	None
Helpers	Elves	Zwarte Pieten
Transportation	Flying reindeer sleigh	Arrives in NL on steam boat called Pakjesboot 12 and then switches to a white horse named Amerigo, which can walk on rooftops and jump far distances
Delivery	Santa delivers the gifts himself via the chimney	Sinterklaas waits on the roof top while his Zwarte Pieten do the work
Gifts	Santa's gifts are made in his elaborate toy factory on the North pole and placed around the Christmas tree	Children traditionally place their shoes around the chimney or stove (or radiator nowadays) and put a carrot or some hay and water nearby for Sinterklaas' horse.

Q: I don't get it. Why are their faces painted black?

A: Please. Save yourself the trouble and don't go asking this question in your Dutch workplace. You won't make any friends.

Q: Wait. Am I allowed to say anything critical about the Sinterklaas tradition?

A: No.

Q: Ok... back to basics then. When is it officially celebrated?

A: Get out your Dutch agenda! Although he makes his first appearance mid-November, Sinterklaas doesn't get into the full swing of things until December 5th.

Q: This is the night for the poem and present stuff, right?

A: Yeppers. On the eve of the 5th (pakjesavond) children place their shoes by the fireplace (although hardly any Dutch homes have them), or by the radiator (how the heck do the presents get through that?) or by the door (for the brighter Dutch children), and eagerly await their presents.

Q: What do they get?

A: Back in more modest times presents consisted of mandarin oranges, chocolate letters (the initial of your first name), chocolate coins or marzipan figures. Nowadays, combine that with full-fledged gift giving, with the average Dutch home spending upwards of 130 EUR on presents.

Q: Why did my boss write me a sarcastic poem?

A: Adults get into the full swing of things by writing witty poems to poke fun (orpublicly chastise) their family or friends, and the poems are often accompanied by a gift exchange (similar to a "Secret Santa"). The poems are often funny, and of course, involve Dutch directness!

Q: This Sinterklaas dude seems pretty familiar. Are you saying the Dutch invented the North American Santa Claus?

A: Sinterklaas-like figures are celebrated in Germany, Switzerland, Austria and Belgium, as well as French Flanders. Scandinavian folklore has a "nisse" character who is also pretty similar. Santa Claus is thought to be a combination of Sinterklaas and the British Father Christmas.

Phew! That should cover the basics! Now go out, eat some pepernoten and speculaas, write some poems, buy some presents, paint your face black and join in the fun!

WHAT OUR COMMUNITY HAS TO SAY

My boyfriend and his family, his friend and his family, are all from Brabant and do the shoe thing the night before Sinterklaas. They wake up on the morning with some small gift in the shoe, like a bag of sweets or some kruidnoten. They don't do placing shoes before then and haven't heard of that. So it really can vary, not sure if it's by region or not. Of course they do also do the presents in a sack thing for the kids, but that is their shoe tradition.

Sarah

This is a great post, but you simply must expand on surprises (pronounced "soo-PREE-zuhs") – that's the elaborate, arts&crafts ("geknutseld" is the word I'm looking for) packages that the Dutch adults make each other for Sinterklaas. Imagine you have a friend who is a truck driver, and you're wrapping his gift, and you thought to yourself "Wouldn't it be great (leuk) if this gift looked like his truck". So you make a cab out of cardboard that opens up to reveal a pipe cleaner engine and has wheels made from the souls of old shoes. Dutch make crazy things like this for each other *every year*! Usual it's done Secret Santa style for frugality's sake, but if you're very special a friend might make you a surprise for Sinterklaas just because.

Steve

I am Dutch (as can be) and I love Sinterklaas. The Sinterklaasfeest is a Dutch tradition that doesn't hurt anyone. If you do feel offended by it, than that is YOUR CHOICE. Fine, make your own choices, you have that right, but don't make it then other peoples' faults.

What I do miss in this specific blog, is the 'Sinterklaasjournaal', which is a special daily news bulletin on national television made for the children, about Sinterklaas, his Pieten and everything that goes on from the moment the Steamboat leaves Spain, up until Sinterklaasavond (dec. 5th) and it is hilarious (for the kids) and sometimes scary (also for the kids, i.e. when something goes wrong and they loose all the presents) but from an adult point of view also ingeniously made, with intricate story lines, that keep your kids on their toes for the duration of this period.

Dutch

Great post; just some additional info on the shoes and the gifts:Traditionally, Dutch kids would put a wooden shoe in front of the fire place, and fill it with hay and a carrot for Sinterklaas' horse. And they'd sing a short Sinterklaas song to ensure that Sinterklaas would show up to fill the shoe. Sinterklaas would ride his horse on the roofs of the houses (no word on how he got there!), and zwarte Piet would go down the chimney to fill the shoes with mandarins, pepernoten or chocolate. Small things; setting the shoe is equivalent to stockings in North America. We would be allowed to set our shoes a few days before the 5th. The real gifts on Pakjesavond would arrive in a burlap bag, usually dropped off at the front door. There would be a loud knock on the door, but Piet would disappear, leaving the bag. The bag is significant, as this is the bag in which zwarte piet takes stoute kinderen (bad children) back to Spain!

Rogier

Having lived 53 years in Canada, we celebrate Sinterklaas each and every year. Boy, are we glad to be far removed from all the hallabaloo that's being raised in my homeland. Sinterklaas always will be a family celebration and has been throughout centuries a heartwarming tradition for young and old. Please, leave political correctness alone for just a day or 10. That's not too difficult?

Marg

Haha I just realized how weird it is that I used to put my shoe in front of the radiator

Femke

#37 BIRTHDAY CALENDAR

May

Su	Mo	Tu	We	Th	Fr
1	2	3	4	5	6
8	9	10	11	12	13
15	16	17	18	19	20
22	23	24	25	26	27
29	30	31	1	2	3

Step into any Dutch home and you will be sure to find one particular household oddity, the Birthday Calendar (*de verjaardagskalender*). And where on earth would you find such an odd item? Well, in the most logical place - the toilet of course! The Dutch are, above all, practical and where else would such an item not be overlooked?

A Dutch person must never forget another Dutch person's birthday. Doing so constitutes a major sin in the Lowlands. Dutch people can happily consult their handy birthday calendar while quietly going about their business on their porcelain throne.

Remember, this calendar is not your everyday calendar. It is not to note your next dental appointment or that dreaded dinner at your colleague's house. The toilet calendar's sole purpose is to record birthdays. Plus it is a perpetual calendar (sans dates or years) forsaking the need to purchase or update it every year. Ah – very efficient and thrifty!

An important word of caution, as tempting as it may seem, it is very important to note that it is never ever appropriate to record one's own name and birth date on another Dutch person's calendar. Doing so would be considered a serious offense. Can't seem to find your own B-day entry? Well, the official relationship-ranking is in, and turns out you're just not as close or as important as you thought you were!

Feeling a tad cheeky? While visiting a Dutch person's home, ask to use the toilet and covertly erase a few entries from the beloved calendar. This action alone is sure to throw the Dutch person's life into complete chaos! *Dat mag niet!*

WHAT OUR COMMUNITY HAS TO SAY

Hahahaha, i never realised that a birthday calendar is typically dutch. also common practice: writing a name of someone you don'nt know that well with a pencil. my ex-mother-in-law wrote my name with a pencil, so she could easilly erase it when necessary. the name of his sisters boyfriend was written down with a pen, because she 'felt that she knew him better'. i must say, she did have good foresight

Charlotte

My father, an American, visited my mom's family in holland after they were married. he had never seen a bday calendar before and he mistakenly thought you were supposed to use the space to write in your name when you used the bathroom.

Jes

An ex-boyfriend of mine was so rude, he wrote his own name on my birthday calendar. Since we broke up I of course don't want to see his name on my calendar anymore. Erasing it won't help; it will still be visible. I therefore tore out the month of July but now I am still reminded of him every time June is past and my calendar goes straight to August. I hate him for spoiling my calendar. It's so arrogant! The only solution is to buy a new calendar.

Goddamnit.I am sweating out of every pore now. Last year I was invited to a birthday of a Dutch guy I know for a while – we are not exactly the type who call each other every few days to catch up or anything... though it's not like we're just mere acquaintances either.
That night, during the peak of my drunkenness, while I was doing No.1 in his toilet, I noticed the calendar and added my name....! Up until this moment I had no freekin' idea it is such a mortal sin! Now I'm considering apologizing to him profoundly, since my bday is approaching... :OJeez!

Almira

This is totally brilliant. As a Dutch I must confess: yes its all true! I hate it if somebody puts his name (yes it happend to often at birthday parties), I want to write in in my own handwriting, not making a mess of my precious art calender. And I must confess I even wrote down a boyfriends name in pencil, judging rightly I would see if he would last...(My present steady boyfriend for years now wants to know if his name actually is in pen.) If it gets to messy, somebody of the family will need to write the whole calender again, let alone find a calender you love so much. Actually I think the calender is also used to express some of your personality... (hence me saying I have an ART calender, see how sophisticated I am?) I love cats, I support a non profit organisation, a very kitsch one so you can see the person is not bourgeous inspite of the old fashioned calender.

Paulien

Just recently my name has been added in the company's (where more than 90% of the employees are Dutch) birthday calendar (albeit the digital version managed by the reception, not in the toilet). Thanks for reassuring me that I've finally made it to the coveted circle. I can finally die happy.

Clarence

#38 NOT WORKING / WORKING

Yes, you read the title correctly. Dutch people like to work and to not work. In fact, they like to not work so much that they've actually become experts at it and are now the best in the European Union at doing so (not-working that is).

The Dutch work the fewest hours of any other nation in the European Union (which pretty much means in the world since we all know that the EU is a pretty cushy place to work). And here you thought that the French were the ones spending their days sipping coffee, shopping for baguettes and playing boules. Well, guess again - the Dutch are pretty darn clever at enjoying the good life.

On average, people in the EU work only 37.5 hours a week, but here in the Lowlands, Dutch people clock-in an average of just 30.6 hours per week! That's almost one whole day less a week than all their other EU neighbours. Let's not even get started on the drastic differences of our friends across the pond! The average North American works between 44-52 hours per week. The difference is truly shocking. Compare 30.6 hours to the low end of an American 44 hour work week and that's a difference of 697 hours per year (or 87 fewer working days)!! Wow. There is no doubt it's the Dutchie who's definitely got a better grasp on work-life balance.

The Dutch on average get 25 days a year vacation time. Whether it is paid holiday time or weekly working hours, the Dutch have managed to have their cake and eat it too!

How, you ask, are the Dutch spending all this free time? Well, my friends, they are certainly enjoying themselves. They are riding their bikes, sitting at cafes discussing the weather, leisurely shopping for drop and hagelslag, enjoying mama/papa dags, eating herring and frolicking in the tulip fields. All jokes aside, the Dutch also top the productivity list in the EU, so something is definitely working and they are having a hell of a good time doing it!

The women, however, appear to be having the best time of all. Many women work part-time and were recently ranked as the "happiest women in the world". It appears they have figured out what we all inherently know is true, working less is simply better. It's a good life in the Lowlands!

WHAT OUR COMMUNITY HAS TO SAY

I've read an article by an American lady who thought that all the Dutch women spend their days with drinking coffee instead of their career. It just pissed me off... Although a lot of women work part-time, to compare this with America is just not right, because I think that in America you have: 'stay at home mums' or 'career women' and no women who work part-time. I really don't know a lot of stay-at-home mums among my friends, but a lot of friends who are mums work part-time.

Priscilla

Sandeman
Ha! This just means we're almost twice as productive as the Americans. Now excuse me while I enjoy the rest of my well deserved free time

Walter
Excuse me but North Americans do not work longer but they are longer at their work.

Harm
Work hard, play hard!

1karla
Dutch women usually work parttime, that explains the low average

Irving
Ha, that's why we are so uptight about being efficient!The more efficient we are, the more we can spend time enjoying ourselves. Looking forward to that long walk on the beach already...

Eric
I am a single Dutch man, so without a partner to share the costs with, yet I still only work 20 hours a week, in a job with 6.5 weeks of holiday a year. I can usually fill those 20 hours by working two slightly longer days, giving me a 5 day weekend. always. how, do you ask? by prioritising.

Piet
Perhaps that is because the Dutch just work more efficient and aren't as money crazed as the rest of the world?!

Ozolief
Better work hard for 30 hours and be productive, then work 53 hours with big breaks and not getting stuff done

Hattie
Living as a Dutch person in the US and moving here after my 30th, I had to make a huge adjustment. Mandatory overtime, are u kidding me. Making me come in on my day off to work. Yes, you'll pay me time and a half, but I rather use my personal time different. When I explain my American co-worker about a CAO they are amazed and then the vacation days we get.Working through my lunch and not eat at all (can't eat at your desk at some places). Mega adjustments for this Dutchie.

#39 COWS THAT SAY BOO
(AND OTHER DUTCH ANIMALS LOST IN TRANSLATION)

THE OTHER DAY, WHILE OUT EXPLORING THE DUTCH COUNTRYSIDE (A.K.A. ENDLESS FIELDS & WINDMILLS) I OVERHEARD A DUTCH MOTHER SPEAKING TO HER CHILD WHILE WE WERE ENJOYING A PIT STOP NEXT TO A FIELD OF COWS. "KIJK", SAID THE MOTHER POINTING TO THE COWS. HER SMALL CHILD THEN BEGAN SHOUTING OUT ENTHUSIASTICALLY, "BOO! BOO! BOOOOO!!" WHY ON EARTH DID THIS CHILD DISLIKE THESE POOR INNOCENT COWS SO MUCH? AND WHO KNEW A 3 YEAR-OLD COULD ALREADY SHOW HIS DISTASTE WITH SUCH ZEALOUS BOO-ING? I KNEW THE DUTCH WERE DIRECT BUT I DIDN'T EXPECT SUCH JADEDNESS FROM A YOUNG CHILD.

Now, now, settle down, of course, the child was not booing the cows. It turns out that Dutch cows actually speak a different language than the familiar North-American dairy cows. While we all know that English-speaking cows say, "moo", hence their nickname, "moo-cows", Dutch-speaking cows prefer to communicate with a slightly more spooky "boo" sound (written as boe in Dutch).

Turns out that Dutch cows aren't the only animals in the Lowlands that speak a different language. Dutch pigs do not say, "oink-oink" like their English-speaking counterparts, but rather, "knor-knor". Dutch roosters do not wake you up with a hearty, "cock-a-doodle-do" but a rather foreign sounding, "kukeleku"!

Dutch cats and dogs seem to be a little more worldly, as they have mastered the international language of "prrrr", "miauw" and "woef woef", with only a slight accent in a Dutch dog's bark.

What is the lesson in all of this my friends? Next time you are attempting to speak to an animal in the Netherlands, make sure you are speaking the same language. That Dutch frog ain't going to understand your "ribbit -ing" and that Dutch rooster is sure to give you a crazy look and shake its head with all your "cock-a-doodle-doo-ing"!!

WHAT OUR COMMUNITY HAS TO SAY

When I lived in America the dogs apparently said bow-wow. Now here in Australia they say woof. There simply is no consistency. We need an international organisation for the standardisation of animal noises…

Mark

In every language is different, in spanish , for us in Venezuela, a rooster will sound "kikirikiiii", a cat would "miau", a dog would "guau guau"

In Brazil dogs says: au, au!

Vania

Antonio

I'm Dutch and live in the UK and have this "argument" with my lovely british misses every time, she won't accept cow's saying "boo". We also don't agree on the noises horses make. Everyone knows a horse says "ieeeeeeeeh-hieee-hiee-hieee" though apperently the English horses say "neej", pronounced as in our "nee". To this day i'm still confused as to why a horse would say neej."here horsey horsey, you want you nice fresh hay ?" NEEJ. "oke fine, i'll take back then!". Crazy British animals…..

Imagine the confusion in our house We are a Dutch family living in the US with a two yr old and a not-quite-4 yr old. We try to teach them *both* animal languages; so here it goes like 'what does a cow say?' daughter: 'Mooooo' Us: 'What do they say in Dutch?' daughter: 'ehhhhhhhh………Boe?' lol. Always a challenge.

Carla

Karim

#40 TINY SINKS WITH ONLY COLD WATER

The mystery of the tiny Dutch toilet sink is a perplexing one. One to which we can't seem to get a straight answer. Why the heck can you only find cold water in these sinks? Why is there only one lonely tap? And why is its only job to provide glacial H2O? What could possibly be the reason for said torture? Why, we ask, why??

We would love to think that there is something else going on here. Something other than the obvious, sheer Dutch "thriftiness" (think cheapness). So please, someone, (anyone) fill in the blanks and give us another plausible explanation. Do the Dutch want to save those extra few pennies rather than having the luxury of washing their hands in warm water?

We can understand the argument that in those charming old canal houses and cozy brown cafés the ancient plumbing does not allow for much alteration. But head to any newly built apartment, restaurant or even one of the modern office towers in Amsterdam's WTC, enter the toilet and you are still destined to find only icy water flowing from those shiny new taps!

Not to mention the size of these tiny toilet sinks. They are normally no more than 10 inches wide and 5 inches deep, which is essentially the perfect size for washing one finger at a time.

Dutch people are apparently not bothered by any of this. In fact, they actually like their 'cold-water-only-tiny-sinks'. Thank you very much! Are Dutch hands simply more resistant to the cold? If you grow up dousing your hands in ice water multiple times a day, do you then no longer feel the cold? And what about basic hygiene? Does cold water really do the trick? Perhaps one day, one particularly powerful Dutch person will experience the joy of washing their hands in warm water while abroad, and will decide there and then to put an end to this madness. This flat, peculiar little country spends a lot of its time being grey and cold and wet and using the toilet sink without gasping from the arctic temperatures would go a long, long way on a cold Dutch winter's day.

WHAT OUR COMMUNITY HAS TO SAY

Hmm, never thought about this untill I read this...Maybe the dutch find washing their hands in cold water more refreshing then in warm water? I personally DON'T like the fact that when I'm at a British airport for example, only warm water comes out of the toilet sinks... What is that about? You can't even take a sip of some refreshing COLD water??? Pure waste of energy all that unneccessary warm water

Twansparant

I'd say that commonly, washing your hands is seen as wasteful and decadent. Don't forget that Calvinistic doctrine forbids most luxuries, which is where a lot of the Dutch thriftiness/cheapness is rooted in.

Michiel

It never occurred to me that you need warm water to wash your hands. For a shower OK, but just your hands can stand a little bit of cold! You non-Dutch people must be a bunch of sissies! What I find strange is wash basins with 2 separate taps: one cold, and one scorching hot. Who's going to put their hands under that?

Emma

To be honest, that's bull. Washing your hands is not wasteful and decadent. Living in the black belt myself, I have never ever heard anybody suggest such a thing. The sink in the downstairs toilet is just too far away from the boiler. The pipes are usually filled with cold water, as you don't keep the hot water running all day for those 15 seconds you wash your hands every so often. By the time the hot water would have finally reached the water tap, you would be done washing your hands.

Henri

That is absolutely true, that has me baffeled too in some foreign bathrooms. I gues the idea is that you have to fill the sink with a mix and wash in the bowl, or so. Rubbing your hands over the ceramics.The topic remembered me on a story of a Dutch immigrant in Canada who for the first time in her life had a indoor bathroom (shower and bathtub). That was not common in the fifties in The Netherlands.It can't be our particular toughness for cold. I was amazed by the freezing temperatures of beer in Canada. Even at -30, Canadians, when they drink a beer, they must experience that brain freeze. That is worse than cold hands.The secret is when a Dutch put his hands in water, their hands don't get wet. The water gets Dutched!

Barry

Ha, I totally agree, there should be hot water too, I mean come on! I am (kinda) used to it now but still dislike it. When I had visitors from America over, a lot of them would actually not wash their hands in the bathroom, but come out to the kitchen and wash them there! ha

Nick

I think it's a combination of 1) cheaper plumming 2) you save water waiting for it to heat up 3) you save gas used for heating up a lot of water (of which you only use a little) 4) you save time when you use only cold water and the most important 5) if the water is too cold for your delicate hands you are "een watje"

Sandeman

We renovated our house that we purchased here in NL, and I insisted on piping in warm water to our WC sink. Our contractor thought we were INSANE. We had a heck of a time finding a faucet small enough to fit the standard Dutch miniscule powder room sink which could provide both hot and cold water, too. We couldn't get a bigger sink because the space is too tiny. Seriously, it was a major hassle! I asked our contractor about the cold water thing and his reply was that he never even BOTHERED washing his hands after using the toilet, but would go do it in the kitchen afterwards. Eww, germs, doorknobs… *shudder* I HOPE this is not the norm! I do have to agree, though, that I think part of it is that so many houses have their boilers up in the attic. If the water has to get all that way just for a quick hand wash, it is a huge waste, and most of us aren't that patient. We lucked out with the boiler in our garage, which is next to the WC (which means it takes forever to get warm water upstairs in the bathroom!). Our contractor thought my wish for a laundry room sink was even more crazy. So crazy, in fact, that he ignored my request and neglected to put the plumbing in at all! He didn't forget – we had talked about it at length. (But there's another post for you: why Dutch builders "like" to not listen to requests from the little wife unless their husbands are there to back them up!).

Jen

Hot water in the bathroom…. In my Dutch opinion that's just ridiculously silly. A total waste of energy and environmentally unfriendly. It takes on average about 7 meters of pipe from the hot-water system to the bathroom tap. The bit of hot water used is usually less than actually gets sucked into the pipe, so you're wasting a LOT of heat for an utterly tiny little bit of 'comfort'. I can get quite annoyed when foreign visitors actually use the hot tap at the sink in the shower room where I brush my teeth. After they've been there, and I want to brush my teeth or wash my hands or some-such I always get greeted by a hot or luke-warm horrible flush. Ugh…Real men use real water. Sissies have to warm it first before their fragile skin can handle these "extremes of nature".*sigh*

Steffen

#41 BEING TALL

Isn't it ironic that the nickname for the Netherlands is the Lowlands. Quite frankly, a more descriptive term would be the Highlands or at least the High-People-lands. If you haven't noticed, Dutch people are tall. Really tall. Tall enough to make even a "normally" tall person feel quite short.

The odd thing here is that the Dutch haven't always been tall. Ever been inside one of Amsterdam's 16th century canal houses? Those tiny doors and quaint low ceilings were indeed built for much smaller people. However, in only a century, Dutch people went from being one of the shortest nations to being the tallest people on the planet! The average Dutch man now measures 1.837 m (6 ft 1 inches) and their lengthy female counterparts are a respectable 1.693 m (5 ft 6 1⁄2 inches).

There are a million and one hypotheses as to why the Dutch are such vertically superior beings. Fabulous health-care? Superior diets? Generous sleep habits? No one knows for sure. But we'll put our money on the big D! Dairy that is. A recent study took an unusual approach by linking the number of cows per capita to the height of a country's people. Whether or not it's the copious consumption of dairy or a winning combination of healthcare, nutrition and living conditions, one thing is true, you will definitely feel much shorter than normal when visiting the Netherlands!

A conclusion might be that all Dutch people have it easy in their lofty towers of height superiority! After all isn't there a positive correlation between height and success? Think again folks, it ain't all fun and games! Nooo... As we speak, the tireless lobbyist group Klub Lange Mensen (Club for the Tall) are busy fighting the fight for enormously tall Dutch people's rights. After all, it ain't easy being tall. Tall Dutch people continually smack their foreheads on doorways, scratch the tops of their heads on low ceilings, and get their lanky legs caught in each others lanky legs while simply trying to walk down the street! Not to mention the inconvenience of air travel, trying to tuck your long, long legs in cramped seats is fraught with peril. The tall Dutch people of the world need help (and apparently anti-growth hormones) and the hard working, self-sacrificing people of the Klub Lange Mensen (KLM) will see that the lanky Dutch get the equalities they deserve.

It ain't all bad news though, KLM's website highlights a recent study on height and happiness; apparently all those smacks on the forehead have beaten the blues right out of the tallest of the tall! Drink your milk children, and you too can enjoy blissful Dutch happiness.

LOOKING DOWN ON THE REST OF THE WORLD
(Average male height in m)

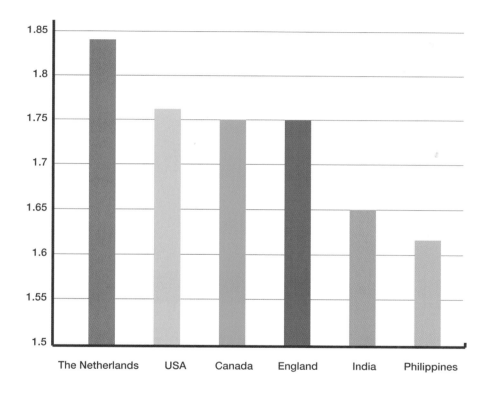

WHAT OUR COMMUNITY HAS TO SAY

It is so funny being 1.78 metres, female, and walking around in Italy. Those people are ridiculously short, quite usefull for seeing over crowds. I'm quite tall even for a dutch girl, but guys tend to be taller than me. Not in Italy though.

Eefje

...but is not so funny being an Italian (short) guy in the Netherlands!

Luca

My dad is 6 foot 6 (slightly over 2 meters), excessively tall for an American. He definitely has to incline his head when he goes through doors. He was an officer in the American navy for twenty years, and when he ported in Amsterdam, he said that there were at least 5-6 other Dutch at the officers club his height or taller. He said it was the most unusual experience for him – not being unusually tall!

Ana

I'm belgian and 6'1I always had trouble finding boyfriends that were taller, or even of equal height... until I started dating dutch guys :p.

Maria

According to the British Medical Journal, the most widely held theories on the excessive height of the Dutch are:1. since the country is so flat, the tallest human predators could observe their prey more easily than shorter predators, so naturally the taller organisms predominated from natural selection,and2. being such a low country, the frequent flooding has tended to eliminate the shorter specimens from the gene pool.

Swhite44

I'am a dutch women who is 1.82 meters (5 feet 11 inches) and compared to my friends i am fairly tall. But I never hit my head on doorways. lol

Rianne

At 1.80 (5'11") I was a quite average woman when I lived in NL – couldn't see over a crowd

Linda

So the message here is....drink your milk and eat you cheese if you want to be a taller person. However not too much otherwise you will bump your head...

Astrid

I'm Dutch and tall. Taller then the average man. I'm 1.86 And I'm happy about it. Even took those pills they mentioned. Imagine how tall I would've been if I hadn't...

Limoentje

My Dutch husband is 202 cm as well and it's just too damned tall. He barely fits in any car to drive and no one can sit behind him because the seat has to be all the way back. He doesn't fit on airplanes. We have to go to specialty shoe stores and pay quite a lot for each pair of shoes. He doesn't fit on hotel beds (his feet hang off the end). He has had knee and back problems his whole life from it. We do have a nice collection of photos from our travels of where he does not fit (things like elevators and bathrooms in other countries). I'm only 162cm and our children are on a projected course to tower over me.

Lost in Nederland

#42 SWEARING WITH DISEASES

ONCE UPON A TIME, MANY YEARS AGO, I HAD JUST MOVED TO THE LOWLANDS AND WAS TAKING MY NEWLY PURCHASED BIKE FOR A RIDE AROUND THE BIG CITY OF AMSTERDAM. OVERWHELMED, I HAPPENED TO ACCIDENTALLY, BUT FAIRLY DRAMATICALLY CUT-OFF ANOTHER DUTCH CYCLIST. THE MAN WAS FURIOUS, STOPPED HIS BIKE AND BEGAN TO CURSE AND YELL LOUDLY AT ME IN DUTCH. NOT SPEAKING ANY DUTCH AT THIS POINT, IT SOUNDED MOSTLY LIKE A MASS OF ANGRY GUTTURAL SOUNDS, BUT ONE WORD IN HIS TIRADE JUMPED OUT AT ME... TYFUS! HUH?? WTF?!? WHAT DID TYFUS (IE: TYPHOID FEVER) HAVE TO DO WITH ANYTHING???

I GOT BACK ON MY BIKE, CONFUSED, AND HEADED TO WORK. OVER A LUNCH OF KARNE MELK AND SANDWICHES WITH HAGELSLAG I TOLD MY DUTCH COLLEAGUE THE STORY. HE DIDN'T LOOK SURPRISED AND CASUALLY REMARKED THROUGH A MOUTHFUL OF BREAD, "YEAH YOU MADE HIM ANGRY, SO HE TOLD YOU TO GO GET TYPHOID". I STARED AT HIM BLANKLY AND MADE A MENTAL NOTE TO DO SOME MORE RESEARCH ON THIS STRANGE CUSTOM...

So now you have it, Dutch people like to swear with diseases. Better yet, they often swear with dreaded diseases from the past. In fact, they go so far as to make angry bold statements wishing these diseases upon you or cursing you with a particular deadly ailment. The more serious your offense, the more serious the disease in question. If you are going to live in the Netherlands for any amount of time, you had better brush up on your knowledge of rare diseases from years gone by. Typhoid, tuberculosis, cholera, small pox, the plague and the more recent Big C (kanker) can all rear their ugly heads.

This "swearing-by-disease" is in fact a unique Dutch trait. No other language has similar curses. It's odd and it's strange and quite frankly, pretty darn harsh. "I hope you get smallpox and die" – certainly doesn't beat around the bush.

Of course, Dutch people have an array of other dirty swear words comparable to other languages. You have your trusty standards like pisvlek (piss stain), lul (dick) and godverdomme (goddamn), but nothing packs a punch quite like "Sterf aan kanker!" (Die of cancer!)

Don't get us wrong. It's not like Dutch people go around all day randomly telling people to drop dead of a certain ailment. But, if you are lucky/unlucky enough to be witness to a serious argument you may happen to hear some 16th century diseases make their way into the conversation.

A CRASH COURSE IN SWEARING IN DUTCH:

Dutch swears can be grouped into 3 main categories:

a) relating to religion
- *godverdomme* (goddamn it)
- *hel* (hell)
- *Jezus Christus* (Jesus Christ), etc.

b) relating to illnesses
- *krijg de kanker* (get cancer)
- *krijg de pest* (catch the plague)
- *krijg de klere* (get cholera), etc.

b) relating to sexuality
- *klootzak* (ball sack - similar to the English swear, "asshole")
- *eikel* (acorn - comparable to the English staple, "dickhead"), etc.

WHAT OUR COMMUNITY HAS TO SAY

My brother gave me a book on my birthday called "Krijg de Vinkentering".It is a list of 1001 curses with background information. Most of the curses mention a disease, but there are also a lot that are somewhat funny.One of my favorites was: Krijg eeuwige jeuk en te korte armpjes. (Get eternal itching and short arms)!

Tim

You're absolutely right about this strange habit, but I need to say one thing: the majority of people don't swear by using the word kanker (cancer). It is considered the roughest and most offensive curse ever and everybody who has developed some level of decency will always avoid this word.

Edel

I'm Dutch and I know a lot of my compatriots use this (cancer) frequently, more so probably in cities. I definitely strongly dislike this – always have and always will.I think it's extremely rude and offensive, and people doing this clearly have no idea how awful a thing it is that they are wishing someone in that moment.

Laura

When I was young, the worst curse or rather insult was "ingeblikte piemelvlees" (canned penis meat) … go figure …

Maikel

We dutch take our swearing very serious. It's so boring telling everyone to go F@#@ themselves.

Sven

I'm dutch and I swear with diseases, but not to wish people to get it, more as something like "you are almost as bad as {disease}"

Tijs

I agree with Tijs, when most people swear with a disease, they don't wish you to have the disease, they more or less compare you to it. I live in the hague where people are actually known (by the rest of the country) for using "kanker" (cancer) as swearing (way too often, I sometimes hear conversations between people using 3-6 cancers in each sentence), but it's not used as a swear that often actually, more as a filler like 'fucking'. Kankerzooi, wat een kankerlijer ben je als je zo'n kankerstreek uithaalt, kanker!loosely translates to:Fuck, what a fuck-face are you, pulling a fucking prank like that….. Fuck!

Martijn

The Dutch sure are a strange breed when it comes to cursing. I myself, being Dutch, never swear with Cancer and tell people off for it. I travel a lot and have never been able to completely explain the nature of Dutch cursing, when people ask. The expression you see on peoples faces when you tell them in your country people swear with Cancer is ridiculous and reminds me, that it is in fact rather ridiculous.

Hestravels

Over the past few years these illness-expletives have made it into positive adjectives, much like 'fuck' in 'fucking nice!'. For example, 'kankerlekker!' means 'fucking tasty/sweet'. Most often used amongst youth and certainly not in polite company.

Sijmen

It's mainly because of the sound of it. Kut, cunt, cock, klote, pik, fuck. They all have the sound of k in it and kanker even has 2!

Gido

#43 SPEAKING IN EXPRESSIONS

THEY'RE OUT OF THE SLEEVE!

I USED TO HAVE A COLLEAGUE WHO ALMOST EXCLUSIVELY SPOKE TO ME IN DUTCH EXPRESSIONS. NOW OF COURSE, SOME WOULD SEE THIS AS CHARMING, PERHAPS EVEN EDUCATIONAL. THE PROBLEM WAS THAT MY COLLEAGUE SPOKE IN DUTCH EXPRESSIONS HAPHAZARDLY TRANSLATED INTO HIS OWN UNIQUE ENGLISH VERSION.

THE RESULT WAS A BIZARRE MIX OF ENGLISH WORDS STRUNG TOGETHER SENSELESSLY HANGING IN THE AIR – AND REQUIRED MY CONSTANT NOD OF APPROVAL/UNDERSTANDING. MANY A MORNING WAS SPENT HEARING ABOUT COWS BEING PULLED OUT OF DITCHES, TALL TULIPS GETTING THEIR HEADS CHOPPED OFF AND MONKEYS. YES, MONKEYS!

There is no doubt that the Dutch love their expressions. Once you start to understand the language you will see that Dutch expressions can be grouped into 3 categories:

1) expressions relating to farm life: these involve the beloved Dutch cows, farmers, fields, windmills, etc.
2) expressions relating to the endearing Dutch weather: these involve wind, rain, sun or sea.
3) expressions that make no sense at all!

The latter is indeed, of course, our favourite. One can only handle so much talk of wind and rain!

Some of the truly bizarre are:
- Als de hemel valt, krijgen we allemaal een blauwe pet
(Translation: If the sky/heaven should fall, we will all be wearing blue caps/hats). Huh?? Say that again??

Or how about stating the obvious:
- Als het regent in september, valt kerstmis in december
(Translation: If it rains in September, Christmas will be in December). So that's why Christmas falls in December e-v-e-r-y year!

Or the always useful:
- Helaas, pindakaas
(Translation:
Oh well, peanut butter).
No explanation needed here,
right? Right?

DOES A COW CATCH A HARE?

You may never be able to wrap your head around some Dutch expressions, but things get even more confusing when Dutch people casually translate one of their own expressions into English and carry on speaking as if it is completely normal. Try keeping a straight face when your colleague announces, "Now the monkey comes out of the sleeve!" or, "You can't make chocolate from it!" You can, of course, ask for an explanation but we've since learned that one often doesn't exist. You, well, just can't make chocolate from it...

To leave you with some words of Dutch wisdom, "He who has butter on his head, should stay out of the sun!" *Got it!?! Good, now carry on!!*

SOME EXAMPLES OF DUTCH EXPRESSIONS

Dutch expression	English translation (+ meaning)
Nu komt de aap uit de mouw	Now the monkey comes out of the sleeve (=*Now the cat is out of the bag*)
Het leven is een pijpkaneel. Ieder zuigt eraan en krijgt zijn deel.	Life's like a candy stick. Everyone sucks on it and gets their share.
Jij weet nooit hoe een koe een haas vangt	Who knows how a cow catches a hare? (=*You never know*)
Ik plak je achter het behang en ga verhuizen	I'll paste you behind the wallpaper and then move away
Zoals de waard is, vertrouwt hij zijn gasten	How the innkeeper is, that's how he treats his guests (=*Ill doers are ill deemers*)
Al draagt een aap een gouden ring, het is en blijft een lelijk ding	Even with a golden ring, a monkey remains an *ugly thing (=you can put lipstick on a pig, it's still a pig)*
Dit slaat als een lul op een drumstel	This hits like a [male genital] on a drum (=it's *bs*)
Helaas, pindakaas!	Too bad, peanut butter

WHAT OUR COMMUNITY HAS TO SAY

It's true. Us Dutch people are so convinced of our extraordinary ability to speak English, we often forget our own language is full of expressions and idioms, and will simply proceed to translate them directly. As a half English person I often come across horribly embarrassing examples. Dutch organisations and businesses will be so convinced of their skill in the English language, they don't even bother to hire a proper translator and instead just do it themselves (this may in part also have something to do with Dutch thriftiness). I recently came across a publication in Amsterdam, geared towards visitors, highlighting all the hotspots and parties in town that week. The articles were so full of Dutch idioms translated directly into English, I cringed with embarrassment.
Dutch people would do well to be more modest about their English abilities, and hire a professional translator every now and then.

Sam

Talk about a great Dunglish example: "I am a dutch undertaker" (ondernemer = entrepreneur) ! Minister van Agt. Hahaha

Cecile

Or as my Dutch mother-in-law said to the head chef of an Oyster Bar in San Fransisco's gay area as she was leaving, at the top of her voice with large arm gestures: "The great cock!"

Lex

What about: Vier en vijf is niet genoeg (Four and Five is not enough). My grandfather used to say this expression ALL the time and I never got it (although I am a Dutchie myself)

Patricia

Lol….too funny that these expressions have made you smile in wonder, fortunately the english expression "when the shit hits the fan" makes much more sence to us then ours do to you. Love this site….keep it up, always makes me feel proud to be Dutch.

Jan

When I was working for GE I used to have great fun literally translating Dutch sayings in English for those Americans, and watch the puzzled expression on their face.E.g. in a casual conversation, observing "It is real branch weather today" (Takkeweer).Still can't help smiling.

Pieter

Another monkey expression: I'm monkeyproud (Ik ben apetrots)

Maarten

To indicate how much i enjoyed reading your posts > it made me miss my 18:00 dinner.

Marcel

My favorite: If your aunt had balls, she would be your uncle. Although I am Dutch, when I was younger I was fairly puzzled by this expression.

Liubi

How about the food is so good, its as if a little angel peed on your tongue or as you begin to eat someone says eat with hooks so you can pull it back up and enjoy it again?

Fred

#44 WHITE LEGGINGS

There are some telltale signs when spring has finally sprung in the Netherlands. The birds chirp, the sun shines and the skies turn an unfamiliar blue colour. People on the street actually smile at each other and fewer elbows are thrown on the metro or in Albert Heijn. When the rainy season comes to an end, the people of the Lowlands are in a good place, a happy place, a place where they feel comfortable enough to wake up in the morning, look into their closets and zestfully throw on their favourite spring outfits.

With the arrival of spring smiles and sunshine one particularly frightful Dutch fashion faux pas rears its ugly head (or should we say "legs"). We've introduced you to the horror of the Dutch man's red pants, but Dutch women are not so innocent. It's time to meet the red pant's ugly step-sister, the white legging!

The white legging is miraculously fashionable in the Lowlands and its presence is disturbingly ubiquitous. They most often can be found coupled with an ill-fitting short denim skirt, brown boots, some sort of Desigual-esque top and that signature red-from-the-box short choppy mullet-like haircut. You know the one!

It is hard to decide if the white legging in itself is so offensive or the sheer number of the pale-legged clones roaming the streets. As a rule, white pants and leggings should be reserved for those working in the health and/or dental sector. They have no place trotting around innocently on the streets.

Things could be worse... At least the trend of 'leggings-worn-without-a-skirt or pants-which-makes-one-think-you-are-looking-at-a-bare-bum', has yet to hit the Netherlands. Head over to the UK or North America and you will see hoards of girls and grown women who apparently forgot to finish dressing before they left the house. Let us pray that this trend doesn't cross the ocean blue... as we know the white legging would take it to an even scarier level.

WHAT OUR COMMUNITY HAS TO SAY

Well Dutch... I think you may categorize these people as either baby-boomers/seniors or people that enjoy listening to "The Toppers" in their free time. In regard to the last category, their taste for clothing is not the only thing that's wrong. Anyway, I find it very amusing however that someone from the Northern American continent is criticizing us Europeans on fashion

Dutch

Yes but this doesn't make this article an invalid critique! They may be a minority but I'm sure there are Americans with good taste. Kisses from Paris (where white leggings are hardly to be seen, yay)

Julia

Lola

@Pauline, if only this would be true. where I work, there is plenty ladies (and men) who earn well, are spending loads of money on their appearance (and very much care about their looks). First ray of sunshine and they r all in their best white (and I dont work in the hospital)

Pauline

O dear, even non-Dutch are picking up on this horrific trend that the least bit of sun= 3/4 white leggings to celebrate the occasion. It's been here for a few years now, and it seems white leggings are here to stay. And unfortunately, the square, shapeless, often too short (as in: above the pudgy knees, for ladies who really should know better but who apparently don't own full-length mirrors) skirt + awful "I'm a mum now so I need an easy hairdo / I'm a mum now and I just don't care anymore" short hairstyle go with it…. *shudders* (btw, 3/4 leggins under a skirt is fine, but NE-VER white!)

Renske

I am Dutch, and I hate the white legging. In my knowledge people wear these because they don't want to show much skin this early in spring/summer (or never). Or the reason can be because the skin has not tanned yet, or otherwise the skin looks more tanned with white clothing (they think). I think that only little girls should where white leggings underneath there dress, so it's not to bare skin. After the age of 10, girls and woman should NOT wear white leggings!!!

Linda

Thank you!! dank je!! for making this problem aware. And its not only the white leggings, its most of all the leggings-as-pants phenomenon. Oh lord those things are everywhere and they make me sick! Seriously people, i can see your underwear and i don't wanna see it… -_-" And then the patterns on those things… they keep getting uglier! (just the tip of the iceberg of horrible fashion. Uggs, crocs, coats with too much fur and coats that look like trash bags or that horrendous patch of too short hair that hipster girls wear lately, just to name a few.

Steffen

HEAR HEAR is all I need to say. HEAR HEAR!!! The ridiculous short hair. The horrific red hair. The disgusting white leggings. The disgraceful footwear. The offending inability to match clothing. It really is something.

#45 BESCHUIT MET MUISJES

By now you've probably gathered that the Dutch are an interesting bunch with some equally perplexing traditions. If you are lucky enough to celebrate the birth of a baby in the Lowlands, be prepared for a culinary "treat". After Dutch women birth their babies, they immediately head to the kitchen, grab some beschuits (a twice baked piece of round toast), slap on a thick layer of butter and adorn it with either pink & white (for a girl) or blue & white (for a boy) sprinkles.

Don't go confusing these sprinkles for hagelslag - nooo - these little guys are called muisjes (yes, mice) and they are candy covered anise (aniseed) seeds. Piles of these crunchy oddities are stacked on plates and served to guests visiting the new babe.

MY FORMER DUTCH BOSS ONCE TRIED, MUMBLING AND STEEPED IN MALE —EMBARRASSMENT, TO EXPLAIN HOW THE TRADITION CAME ABOUT. THROUGH HIS MUMBLED SPEECH I GATHERED SOMETHING ABOUT ANISE SEEDS SHRINKING A WOMAN'S... ERRR... LADY PARTS (WOMB, THAT IS). OF COURSE THIS DIDN'T EXPLAIN WHY THE DUTCH SERVED IT TO THEIR GUESTS BUT I THOUGHT I HAD BETTER END THE CONVERSATION AND SPARE HIM ANY ADDITIONAL HUMILIATION.

ACCORDING TO OUR GOOD FRIEND MR. WIKIPEDIA, THE ANISE IS THOUGHT TO BE GOOD FOR "STIMULATING LACTATION", RETURNING THE UTERUS TO ITS "NORMAL SIZE" AND WAS "PURPORTED TO SCARE AWAY EVIL SPIRITS." IT'S GOOD TO HEAR THE TRADITION IS ROOTED IN SOME SORT OF LOGIC, AND IT TURNS OUT MY BOSS WAS ON THE RIGHT TRACK!

Dutch people apparently can't come to a consensus as to why these colourful anise seeds are called Muisjes. Some claim it is due to their shape - the anise seed when covered in sugar has a small tail and thus resembles a mouse. Others claim they were called "mice" in reference to the rodent's abundant fertility. Regardless of the origin, the name stuck... and the rest is history.

ORANGE MUISJES WERE SOLD EN-MASSE
FOR ONE WEEK IN DECEMBER 2003
TO HONOUR OF THE BIRTH OF
CROWN PRINCESS AMALIA

WHAT OUR COMMUNITY HAS TO SAY

Being Dutch I grew up with the tradition of eating 'beschuit met muisjes' whenever a baby was born and never really thought about why there were called muisjes. But one day I had a better look at one of the individual muisjes and noticed the stem of the anise seed is sort of sticking out of the blue or pink coating, which makes it look like a muisje. Some searching on the internet confirmed this was indeed the reason for calling these sprinkles muisjes. In my family we also eat 'beschuit met muisjes' on Christmas day; I think it's a lovely tradition, but haven't met anyone else yet who does the same.

Kristel

They are called muisjes because they look like mice droppings. tasty mice droppings..

Reefer

They are called muisjes because usually a little 'tail' of the aniseed sticks out, making the sprinkles look like abstract mice.

Pookie

Exactly! Because of the little tails!

Marieke

I found out a while ago why we have the tradition of eating 'muisjes' (sugar covered anise seeds) when a child is born: the anise stimulates the milkglands in a woman's body, so she gives more milk to her baby! Which was the reason why my American friends refused to eat it, hahaha!!!

Esther

And then there are gestampte muisjes. I'm Dutch (and now live in Texas) and when my American boyfriend (now my husband) first took a bite of an open-faced sandwich with gestampte muisjes, he almost choked. The powder is so light and we hadn't warned him not to breathe in while holding the sandwich to his mouth…

Barbara

My Oma used to bring me beschuit met muisjes in bed whenever I visited her. Fond memories.

Derek

This is what I miss most! But just so you know, we eat the 'muisjes' the entire year.

Susanne

#46 SUSPICIOUS SPREADS

The words "Dutch" and "lunch" are sure to lead to disappointment. There is no way around it, Dutch lunch is a very sorry affair. It involves a lot of dairy, a lot of bread and a lot of smearing. The sooner you can get used to eating bread smeared with some indiscernible lumpy matter, confusingly referred to as "salade" or "filet", the better.

For a country generally lacking in culinary creativity, the Dutch are actually incredibly creative in the "sandwich spread department". They have managed to turn all sorts of perfectly edible food into lumpy, blended goo. You can always find your standard egg salad or tuna salad sandwich spreads, but the Dutch have kicked it up a notch and invented all sorts of new gooey concoctions.

Why not try some "*kip sate salade*" (pureed chicken and peanut sauce), or some "*garnalen knoflook salade*" (blended shrimp and garlic smear) or "*farmersalade*" (blended farmer??). All involve copious amounts of mayonnaise just to ensure that you also consume 99% fat and 1% goodness on your whole wheat bread.

If these salades are not your cup of tea, you always have your trusty selection of smeerkaas to fall back on. (Any female native English-speaker will tell you that the word 'smear' should only be reserved for the dreaded annual doctor's appointment... and certainly not in the context of cheese!)

Smear-cheese isn't your thing either? Well, have no fear, we've saved the best for last, Filet Americain. Filet americain is the quintessential nasty Dutch spread.

Hungry? Just take a juicy handful of raw beef or horse meat, throw it into a blender, add some seasoning, maybe a bit of onion and blend away until it's a smooth raw pink paste and then (you guessed it) smear it on your bread! Anyone in the mood for parasites, with a side of E.Coli or Salmonella?

Yes, sometimes fact is stranger than fiction, The Dutch do indeed like/love this stuff! *Eet smakelijk!*

WHAT OUR COMMUNITY HAS TO SAY

The funny thing is, when you choose a "salad" such as the goo described above, they actually think it's the healthy option, because the alternative, is goo deep fried in the form of a kroket…which I admit, are actually delicious on bread.

Matt

I begrudgingly admit that I put my American squeamishness and paranoia aside for filet American. I LOVE filet American, tapeworms and E. coli risks be damned. Onions, mayo, and raw seasoned beef FTW!

Laura

To my observation, most of Europeans have warm meal on their plates for lunch;)

Alexandra

This post is much over-rated and typically American .Dutch lunch is not so bad as is described.Everything "we" or "us" Europeans" have in the lunch department still beats everything from the USA !!!Taste and health wise…And that is a world known fact!(a country where at least 70% is overweight … no offence by saying this) Before you try to trash(that's how i see it!) "the Dutch" beter get your facts straight about them or take a good look at your own country!

Vincent

HAHA! Just had lunch in China.. They served me cold duck tong and pig ears… Give me my SMEERKAAS!!!

Jaap

I actually like some of the salads, but more komkommer and farmer salads (and they aren't "blended" like the other ones). I love filet americain. I have never once EVER been sick from filet and I've lived here in NL for almost 19 years. I do think the Dutch could eat more than just boterhammen, but hey, I am not a bread person (the horror! I know!). It's getting better; we have much more choice these days in the cantine. I'll stick with a maaltijdsalade, dankjewel! you want to talk gross (Dutch) foods… let's discuss the frikadel!!!

Renée

American guy who lived, worked and loves Holland here – a few comments:- it only befits the zuinig aspect of Dutch life that these salads contain the least of the most expensive items like shrimp, etc and the most of god-knows what!- in Holland (EU overall) food recalls are a slim fraction of what happens in the US so these, tho high on the "EWWWW Factor" are safe. Conversely you would be taking your life in your hands eating such things in the USA where some over 100 million tons of food are recalled every year for e.coli, salmonella, etc .

Richard

Yummy. I took to the spreads living in Holland. I love them all

theflyawayamerican

Damn, now I'm hungry…

For the Dutch; cooking and eating are interruptions in the workday to be gotten over with as quickly as possible, so as to return to more productive pastimes, None of that French or Italian "lounging about" over a thoughtfully prepared meal.

Lawrence

I love the fact that fat foreigners comment on our food consumption. Dutch are the longest, one of the healthiest, happiest and joyful people in the world and thats due to what we eat too. Our food is made up from dozens of cultures and consists of many tastes and forms. Foreigners just enjoy the huge amount of choice!

Bastiaan

Well what are you supposed to eat for lunch then? I guess we just don't know any better.

Gido

Try things like vegetables, meat and fish that actually look like what they once were instead of processed goo-sauce or splat salad from a Johma tub.

Michael

#47 DOE NORMAL

There is no denying that Dutch people like normalcy. The Dutch expression "Doe normaal" roughly translates to "Just be normal already". Doe normaal is the kind of statement your Grandma might say to you in church if you were blasting Hip Hop tunes from your iPhone during the Lord's Prayer. But in the Lowlands your Grandma is the least of your problems. This time it's your Dutch partner saying it, your colleagues thinking it, the shopkeepers whispering it under their breath, and your neighbours tsk tsking about it behind your back.

So, just what does "being normal" actually mean in the Netherlands? Well, the easiest way to define acceptable Dutch behaviour is to list the biggest offenders of "non-normalcy".

They are, in no particular order:

1. bragging
2. showing off or acting pretentious
3. discussing money (especially, how much you have)
4. showing overt public displays of anger or emotion
5. not following the ever-important unwritten rules and regulations
6. acting or being perceived to be "weird", "different", "disobedient" or "foreign".

If you are out and about in the Lowlands and you hear the phrase *"Niet normaal."* uttered with contention under someone's breath, you can safely assume you have crossed some invisible boundary of socio-cultural norms. Congratulations are in order as your behaviour has been officially deemed "not normal". We'd advise retracing your steps to see exactly where the fuss began – or – simply getting on with your day and accepting it as a first of many cultural blunders to come.

So, as you can see, Dutch people like normalcy and it can be proven. When asked to define the Dutch national character, 9 out of 10 people quoted, *"Doe maar gewoon, dan doe je al gek genoeg"*. Translation: "Just act normal, that's crazy enough!!

WHAT OUR COMMUNITY HAS TO SAY

Rembrandt

Don't let the door of Holland hit your ass on the way out.

Marjoleine

You nailed it! It's the one quality I can't stand about my culture. The Dutch preach diversity but judge everyone who doesn't fit the average mold to be "niet normaal". Oh well, no place is perfect…

Sabrina

They are super nosey too! A friend of mine had the raad voor kinderbescherming called on her because during a time of deep depression her curtains (god forbid) were mostly kept closed and her lawn wasn't mowed to the perfect 1 inch height,

Wee

Well, as I'm working in mental health care I know that people in a depression often have difficulties giving their children the attention they need. The Raad voor Kinderbescherming is often seen as the institution that takes children away, which is a large misunderstanding and that is only done as a very last resort. They aim to help parents become better parents and it's not a bad thing to check up on someone when they're depressed and a parent.

Linda

Yup we're all about normalcy here. But you could also interpret "normal" as healthy, reasonable, considerate, appropriate behaviour etc. So if you do something stupid and someone shouts "doe normaal", it could just mean "behave", or "think of the children" Or someone could say "vind je dat normaal?" (do you think that's normal?) as in: do you actually think that behaviour is appropriate? It has a slightly different connotation than just being "normal" as in average, or the same as everyone else.

Erik

"Doe normaal" is perhaps better interpreted as "Stop acting crazy" than "be normal".

I think this is something to do with living with a lot of people in a very small space. It's much easier to accept behaviour that irritates when you can put distance between yourself and what irritates you. If someone is behaving "niet normaal" on a tram packed with people, it is very annoying indeed. Also, I think Japan has a similar rigid code of conduct that you shouldn't deviate from. The typically dutch part of it is the belligerence... We dutch are very belligerent sometimes! BTW, love the site, I have never in my life felt so dutch! I actually do recognize lots of the behaviour you describe in myself, including but not limited to: agenda's, birthday calender in the toilet and getting irritated by someone (family) forgetting my birthday, trakteren, going camping enzovoorts..

Sas

lol
My mom sometimes said 'doe normaal, dan doe je al gek zat' , 'be normal, that weird enough already'

Thammy24

Another well known Dutch saying: 'Steek je kop niet boven het maaiveld', I don't know the exact translation, but It means something like you mustn't draw the attention/stand out of the crowd.'Anders word je kop eraf gehakt'. Otherwise you will be punished.

Flip

I think Dutchies are a pretty tolerant bunch. They don't care who you are, what you believe in, whoever you wish to sleep with, as long as they, we, aren't confronted with it. Which isn't the same as not accepting differences; it just isn't socially accepted to show off said differences. 'Doe maar normaal,' is, in my opinion, telling someone that what they are doing isn't necessarily wrong, it's just inappropriate.

Yos

Niet normaal this article

mastert

#48 DELAYING MARRIAGE

A DUTCH FRIEND OF MINE JUST GOT ENGAGED. SHE'S IN HER MID-THIRTIES AND HAS BEEN WITH THE DUTCH MAN IN QUESTION FOR MANY YEARS. SO IT SHOULDN'T REALLY COME AS SUCH A SURPRISE. BUT IT DID. IT DID. BECAUSE SHE'S BEEN LIVING WITH THIS GUY FOR OVER 10 YEARS AND THEY'VE HAD 2 CHILDREN TOGETHER (NOT TO MENTION A FAIRLY PRICEY DOWNTOWN AMSTERDAM APARTMENT). SO WHY WOULD MARRIAGE SUDDENLY BE SO IMPORTANT NOW?

You know that old schoolyard rhyme: Sally and Ryan sitting in a tree, k-i-s-s-i-n-g. First comes love, then comes marriage, then comes Sally with a baby carriage. Well, in the Lowlands, it seems the rhyme somehow got reversed over time. Countless Dutch get around to the marriage part AFTER already having the love and the baby carriage(s).

The highly complex mathematical formula here in the Lowlands appears to be: attraction + love + buying a house together + having babies = marriage. Of course, ultimately the order of this stuff doesn't really matter. But seeing rational, down-to-earth grown up Dutch women soooo overwhelmingly excited about their romantic proposals and upcoming nuptials - with men whom they've woken up beside for years - is quite the sight!

We've said it once and we will say it again, Dutch people like to do things differently. So it shouldn't come as a shock that they've somehow gone and reversed the age-old order of love and marriage. Is it just to spice things up? Or is it to buck convention? Or is it another form of Dutch practicality and pragmatism? We haven't figured it out yet, but maybe you can!

WHAT OUR COMMUNITY HAS TO SAY

Just let me say Dutch people are kinda great. This Spaniard just hope my Dutchman won't wait too much long to get engaged

Spaniard

Since moving to Nederland I have been amazed at the large number of parents who are well into their 30s, 40s or even later and yet have young children. I think that is a great phenomenon, because so many married couples in the US begin having children when they are too young, and the stress overwhelms them. Delaying marriage and child-bearing makes for more stable families.

Michael

There really is no need to get married, as long as you don't have kids or a house together. That's the rational part: the contract of matrimony is only useful when you reach that level of intertwinedness. But indeed: there's even less of a reason not to throw a great party once you do!

Jules

May I add to everyone's comments, that it's really just more practical to get married once you have kids and a house. You already know you're committed anyways (so, no risk there) and it only makes sense then to get married for financial reasons. But that doesn't mean you can't throw a gezellig feestje and have a romantic wedding.

Anna

I don't see the big deal. My husband and I lived together for over seven years before we got married. We agreed no children until we were ready for marriage. Weddings are time consuming and stressful, not to mention it costs quite a bit. You really want the relationship to work if your going to go through all that and you never really know a person until you live with them, so Dutch people sort of have the right idea I think.

Jess

Its very easy you dont want kids? get out your not married.

Daan

Was that English? Yikes. Grammar + spelling = important. Vooral als je een ''punt duidelijk wil maken in een andere taal.

Floor

It is so true! I happened to work with many Dutchmen, and this story repeats over and over again. I thought it was some particular characteristics, but now I see that this is quite a common phenomenon really…Thank you!

Unordinary

#49 INFILTRATING ENGLISH

Dutch people should be proud. Very proud. For such a tiny little country, they've managed to successfully penetrate the English language. Have you ever noticed how often the Dutch are referenced in English expressions? No? Well, below is a little list to get you started:

Dutch bargain: a bargain made when you are too drunk to know better (first recorded in 1654)

Dutch defence: a legal tactic whereby you rat someone out in order to get off free (first recorded in 1749)

Dutch courage: booze induced bravery (first recorded in 1826)

Dutch gold: a cheap gold-like alloy

Going Dutch/ Dutch treat: where everyone pays for their own meal (so essentially no "treat" at all)

Dutch widow: a prostitute

As you can see, the majority of English expressions using the word "Dutch" aren't too positive. Most of them in fact, pack quite the punch and seem to foster more than a little animosity. Why so? Well, the Dutch had quite a prolific history of seafaring, trade and war. The Anglo-Dutch wars of the 17th and 18th centuries resulted in the Brits not feeling too much love towards the Dutchies and vice versa. These phrases reflected the opinion of that time when the Dutch were considered to be a slightly boozy, slightly cheap folk that were not to be trusted.

Of course, I will be the first to admit that some of these phrases still do make perfect sense. Take "Dutch Uncle" for instance:

Dutch uncle: "a term for a person who issues frank, harsh, and severe comments and criticism to educate, encourage, or admonish someone. Thus, a "Dutch uncle" is a person who is rather the reverse of what is normally thought of as avuncular or uncle-like (which would be indulgent and permissive)."

Try being "not normal" on some occasion, and the whole country might suddenly feel like it's populated by Dutch Uncles!

Don't forget to take a swig of Dutch courage tonight before you pull a Dutch oven on your sweet-heart (and no, we ain't talking about the cooking pot)!

WHAT OUR COMMUNITY HAS TO SAY

I had never heard of the term "Dutch oven" (and I'm Dutch), until some Australian friends explained it to me (though not until they stopped laughing after finding out I was Dutch). And then they asked ME where the saying comes from! How am I supposed to know! You funny English-speaking people are the ones doing it, you must've named it also! Hmpf. Dutch oven.

Geraldine

I'm a Dutch uncle. Ome Ronny, in fact. I teach my English-Turkish nieces right from wrong in the proper way. No English teacher has the balls to do so, so it's left to me. Quite right too!

Ronny

The first noun in the Oxford English dictionary is actually Aardvark...(a Dutch word, derived from Afrikaans (Cape Dutch). In fact many of the Dutch words that made it into the English dictionary...actually came from South African Dutch (Afrikaans).

Chris

And my favorite: you're talking Double Dutch (hard to understand).

Marlies

I think you forgot the best one "Dutch Bingo" You start by asking where they work, or where they live, or where they go to church and eventually you will find someone that you know that they may know or someone that may know the same person that you knew of that your person either knew or may have known someone else that may have known the original person or at least had known someone that they thought probably knew the person that you thought you might have known or at least their acquaintance had heard of that other person and there you have it. 'Dutch Bingo"

Squash11

How about dubble dutch? Having sex with the protection of a condom and the pill!

Eveline

that's called being smart

Surrey

Funny how apparently it is okay for English speakers to use these xenophobic phrases. Can you imagine the outrage should the Dutch language contain such expressions? I even read rants by Americans about an innocent phrase like "Amerikaanse fuif".

Tim

#50

VISIT OUR FACEBOOK PAGE

WWW.FACEBOOK.COM/
STUFFDUTCHPEOPLELIKE

AND SEND US A MESSAGE
WITH YOUR ENTRY
(300-450 WORDS).

DO YOU HAVE
THE MISSING
STUFF DUTCH PEOPLE LIKE
ITEM TO COMPLETE OUR LIST?

STUFF DUTCH PEOPLE LIKE

STUFF DUTCH PEOPLE DON'T LIKE
TOP 10

1 BEING MISTAKEN FOR GERMAN

2 GERMANS

3 FOREIGNERS CRITICIZING ZWARTE PIET

4 POLITICAL CORRECTNESS

5 RAIN ON QUEEN'S / KING'S DAY

6 BICYCLE RIDING TOURISTS (OR TOURISTS IN GENERAL)

7 EATING DINNER AFTER 6PM

8 STABLE GOVERNMENT

9 ACTING "UN-NORMAL"

10 GERMANS

STUFF DUTCH PEOPLE DON'T LIKE

"Foreigners thinking there is nothing more to the Netherlands then Amsterdam. Also people from Amsterdam who think there is nothing more to the Netherlands then Amsterdam." - Arjanne

"The general opinion on germans has changed drastically the last 10 years. Germans are now cool." - Joost

"Running into other Dutchies when on a holiday." - Colinde

"Calling the Netherlands "Holland" " - Jip

"Having to pay for something and discovering afterwards that they could have it for a cheaper price." - Sara

"Oliebollen & pepernoten being sold TOO EARLY!" - Julie

"I'm half Dutch/German, I'm at a constant battle with myself!" - Ronnie

"Extremely hot weather for more then 2 days." - Dennis

"Having to pay for Mayo and/or ketchup!" - Lynn

HOW DUTCH ARE YOU? QUIZ

1. How many bicyles do you own? ☐ A) none ☐ B) 1 - 2 ☐ C) 3+

2. What's your favourite breakfast food? ☐ A) Cereal ☐ B) Bread with cheese
☐ C) Bread with Hagelslag

3. Your colleague comes to work with a new haircut which clearly doesn't suit her.
☐ A) You tell her the haircut looks great
☐ B) You don't say anything
☐ C) You tell her the haircut doesn't suit her and that she looked better with the old sytle

4. You meet a friend who you haven't seen in awhile.
☐ A) You shake his/her hand
☐ B) You give them hug
☐ C) You greet them with cheek kisses

5. How many different uses of the word "lekker" can you think of?
☐ A) 1 - 2
☐ B) 3 - 5
☐ C) 6+

6. A friend asks you to meet up for drinks or dinner.

☐ A) You like being spontaneous and agree on a date/time in the next week

☐ B) You tentatively give him/her a date/time but confirm later after checking your agenda at home.

☐ C) You pull out your agenda and propose a time slot that is available (most likely at least 2 weeks from now)

7. Do you own a pair of red or yellow pants?

☐ A) Hell no!

☐ B) Of course!

☐ C) Yep - one of each!

---

8. Your thoughts on Zwarte Piet:

☐ A) You think it might be a good idea to change the tradition to something that makes everybody happy

☐ B) You don't understand the fuss. He's just black because he came through the chimney! People need to relax.

☐ C) Zwarte Piet is a beloved tradition for children. Anyone who thinks otherwise should get over it, or go somewhere else!

---

9. Which people do you find the most annoying?

☐ A) Belgians

☐ B) Americans

☐ C) Germans

---

10. How much dairy do you consume per week?

☐ A) Not that much

☐ B) I eat cheese or drink milk a couple times a week

☐ C) I love milk and cheese and have it everyday

---

11. What's your idea of a nice vacation?

☐ A) Resort in Mexico

☐ B) Hiking trip in France

☐ C) Camping at a gezellig campground

---

12. What do you like on your fries?

☐ A) Salt & Vinegar

☐ B) Just ketchup

☐ C) Mayo (Frietsauce) or sate

13. You're on vacation in America and you walk into a clothing store.
The employee behind the counter says "Hi! How are you?"

☐ A) You reply "Great, how are you?"

☐ B) You're a bit unsure what to say, but you give a short, honest answer

☐ C) It makes you uncomfortable and you think its a bit fake.

---

14. How do you remember people's birthdays?

☐ A) From memory

☐ B) In your agenda/ Facebook

☐ C) Birthday calendar in my toilet

---

15. What do cows say?

☐ A) Moo

☐ B) Moo or Boo

☐ C) Only Boo

---

16. How tall are you?

Men ☐ A) <1.7m   Women ☐ A) <1.6m

☐ B) 1.7-1.8   ☐ B) 1.6-1.7

☐ C) 1.8m+   ☐ C) 1.7m+

---

17. What's the best order of the following?

☐ A) Marriage, Mortgage, Baby

☐ B) Mortgage, Marriage, Baby

☐ C) Mortgage, Baby, Marriage

---

18. If you had to choose one final dinner, what would it be?

☐ A) Burger & fries

☐ B) Kip sate

☐ C) Pannekoeken

19. As a kid what was your favourite day of the year?

☐ A) Christmas

☐ B) Your birthday

☐ C) Sinterklaas

20. When you think of Zwarte Piet, you feel?

☐ A) Confused and/or uncomfortable

☐ B) Good but with slight hestitation

☐ C) Warm & fuzzy - a wonderful childhood memory

Your total : ⬚

For A give yourself 0 points
For B 10 points
For C 20 points
Add up all your points_____ / 400 = your Dutchness %

HOW DUTCH ARE YOU?

You are clearly not Dutch and never will be! Give up! — less than 20%

There is hope for you to one day become a true Dutchie — between 20% - 40%

Heel goed jonge (of meisje)! You can proudly call yourself Dutch! — between 40% - 60%

You have orange blood and are a prime example of a proud *autochtone!!* — between 60% - 80%

Ok, there is something called "being too Dutch". Perhaps a little travel would do you good! — 80%+

ACKNOWLEDGEMENTS

Thank you to Elisha Leo, our incredible designer, for bringing this book to life. You were amazingly patient with all of our requests and managed to convey exactly what we had hoped for.

Thank you to my fabulous friends and family. You know who you are, and you are loved.

Thank you to Chuck for being my very first ally in this foreign land. You are forever missed.

Thank you to Auntie Connie for always believing in us and our zany ideas.

Thank you to Kyle for laughing at me and my jokes for the past 33 years. If only you think I'm funny, then that's good enough.

Thank you to Mom & Dad for everything you are and have ever done.

Thank you to Kaia for choosing me as your mother. I hope you learn as much from me as I have already learned from you.

And last but not least, thank you to the man who made this all possible. Your name should be on the cover (and on every page for that matter). All I did was write the blog but you made everything else happen. Thank you for being my incredible partner in life, love and business. Every day with you is fun.

ABOUT THE AUTHOR

Colleen Geske is the author of the popular blog *'Stuff Dutch People Like'*. She is originally from Winnipeg, Canada and has lived in Europe since 2004. When not busy writing, Colleen spends her days as a communications and social media consultant. Colleen holds a Bachelor of Commerce (Honours) degree in International Business and Marketing from the University of Manitoba. She currently lives in Amsterdam with her family.

• •

PHOTO CREDITS & ATTRIBUTION

Page	Creator	Source	License type
3	Amsterdamized	http://www.flickr.com/photos/mindcaster-ezzolicious/3292681367/	CC BY SA 2.0
4	John N.		Creator permission
12	Nosha	http://www.flickr.com/photos/nosha/3686335361/	CC BY SA 2.0
24	Smabs Sputzer	http://www.flickr.com/photos/10413717@N08/6957184727/	CC BY 2.0
28	Richard Matthews	http://www.flickr.com/photos/richardofengland/6996622846/	CC BY 2.0
36	hisa fujimoto	http://www.flickr.com/photos/71827087@N00/130685245/	CC BY SA 2.0
39	Free Photo Fun	http://www.flickr.com/photos/79818573@N04/8212037374/	CC BY 2.0
43	Chris	http://www.flickr.com/photos/35995738@N00/7764234402/	CC BY SA 2.0
52	David van der Mark	http://www.flickr.com/photos/d_vdm/9016705353/	CC BY SA 2.0
61	Hans Pama	http://www.flickr.com/photos/hanspama/4121311445/	CC BY 2.0
62	Hans Splinter	http://www.flickr.com/photos/archeon/5214550043/	CC BY ND 2.0
68	Martijn van Exel	http://www.flickr.com/photos/rhodes/6873340785/	CC BY SA 2.0
70	Will Clayton	http://www.flickr.com/photos/21756912@N00/5045502202/	CC BY 2.0
71	Petra de Boevere	http://www.flickr.com/photos/meisjevandeslijterij/6530491189/	CC BY 2.0
74	Tavallai	http://www.flickr.com/photos/tavallai/5492648353/	CC BY ND 2.0
75	Martin Lewison	http://www.flickr.com/photos/milst1/5505578176/	CC BY SA 2.0
83	Christian Van Der Henst S.	http://www.flickr.com/photos/cvander/1371294553/	CC BY 2.0
91	bertknot	http://www.flickr.com/photos/bertknot/8375254125/	CC BY SA 2.0
101	Leo Vogelzang	www.fotoleovogelzang.nl	Creator permission
105	Matsuki Sophia van Coevorden		Creator permission
108	petur r	http://www.flickr.com/photos/53550377@N03/5408020171/	CC BY SA 2.0
111	Russell Neches	http://www.flickr.com/photos/rneches/240855537/	CC BY 2.0
113	John Benson	http://www.flickr.com/photos/j_benson/3527566157/	CC BY 2.0
122	Vinicius Pinheiro	http://www.flickr.com/photos/vineco/7138647219/	CC BY SA 2.0
123	Antonio Olmedo	http://www.flickr.com/photos/olmed0/7129474153/in/photostream/	CC BY SA 2.0
128	Tavallai	http://www.flickr.com/photos/tavallai/5459343031/	CC BY ND 2.0
133	Andreas Kohn	http://www.flickr.com/photos/15341182@N00/6363067651/	CC BY 2.0
142	Ino Paap	http://www.flickr.com/photos/inopaap/2821534852/	CC BY 2.0
152	Simon Elgood	http://www.flickr.com/photos/simon_elgood/3912173122/	CC BY ND 2.0
161	Paul Stenvenson	http://www.flickr.com/photos/pss/3309408487/	CC BY 2.0
165	Mario Zapateria	http://www.flickr.com/photos/oneras/8089372361/	CC BY SA 2.0
168	Nanimo	http://www.flickr.com/photos/20286921@N00/2506752028/in/photolist-4PvL3y-4TwCAf-5ME8Vi-6skaDR-6spkGN-6uZqu8-6v4zHW-6VD2Ev-7uTYm5-am8TFa-7LaL63-86ozEG	CC BY 2.0
171	Kyle Taylor	http://www.flickr.com/photos/95672737@N00/589550663/in/photolist-U6ASB-4wSNL1-5vvqZJ-5CxFVL-5YENFz-6yAmJW-dMdhhu-aUjZQK-gdqCav-bBavJj-979vGR-ejvhQ7-bvoU6u-dZQ4wk-edQQr6-efomjt-dwJJqc-ajyCLu-ahJcZP	CC BY 2.0
179	Jeff Belmonte	http://www.flickr.com/photos/72236935@N00/15921928	CC BY 2.0
183	Patrick Spinney	http://www.flickr.com/photos/patspinney/9765691836/	CC BY 2.0
195	Pim Ras		Creator permission

CC = Creative Commons license/BY = Attribution/SA = ShareAlike/ND = no derivative works
For more information about creative commons licenses visit http://creativecommons.org/licenses/